EX LIBRIS

This is a painter from Skagen.

Bressler

BRINGING IT HOME®
SWEDEN

BRINGING IT HOME®
SWEDEN

THE ULTIMATE GUIDE TO CREATING THE FEELING OF SWEDEN IN YOUR HOME

CHERYL MACLACHLAN

WITH BO NILES

PHOTOGRAPHY BY
IVAN TERESTCHENKO

FROM THE BRINGING IT HOME® SERIES

CLARKSON POTTER/PUBLISHERS
NEW YORK

To Fred, Juniper, and Artiguillon,

FOR THEIR LIFE-AFFIRMING WAYS.

ALL MY LOVE,

Cheryl

PUBLISHED BY CLARKSON POTTER/PUBLISHERS, 201 EAST 50TH STREET, NEW YORK, NEW YORK 10022. MEMBER OF THE CROWN PUBLISHING GROUP.

RANDOM HOUSE, INC. NEW YORK, TORONTO, LONDON, SYDNEY, AUCKLAND
HTTP://WWW.RANDOMHOUSE.COM/

CLARKSON N. POTTER, POTTER,
AND COLOPHON ARE TRADEMARKS OF CLARKSON N. POTTER, INC.

PRINTED IN CHINA

DESIGN BY DONNA AGAJANIAN

LIBRARY OF CONGRESS CATALOGING-IN-PUBLICATION DATA
MACLACHLAN, CHERYL.
BRINGING IT HOME—SWEDEN : THE ULTIMATE GUIDE TO CREATING THE FEELING OF SWEDEN IN YOUR HOME / CHERYL MACLACHLAN WITH BO NILES; PHOTOGRAPHY BY IVAN TERESTCHENKO.—1ST ED.
INCLUDES INDEX.
1. INTERIOR DECORATION—SWEDEN. 2. HOUSE FURNISHINGS—SWEDEN. 3. COOKERY, SWEDISH. I. NILES, BO. II. TITLE.
TX311.M2355   1997
645'.09485—DC20   96-26002

ISBN 0-517-70783-7

10   9   8   7   6   5   4   3   2   1

FIRST EDITION

ACKNOWLEDGMENTS

As an American woman traveling and working in Sweden, I was overwhelmed by the warmth and generosity of the Swedish people. At every turn a helping hand and a winning smile were extended. There are many people I would like to name specifically, but first I would like to offer special thanks to:

Anders and Veronica Öhman, who all but officially adopted me while I created this book. With boundless grace and kindness, Anders and Veronica put a roof over my head and surrounded me with a network of love and support.

Lukas and Gun Bonnier, who not only helped me to find some of the exquisite houses pictured in this book, but also first welcomed me into their home in the archipelago eight years ago and opened my eyes to the splendors of Sweden. A particular gratitude also goes to Lukas for teaching me how to count in Swedish so that I could understand my answering machine messages.

In countless ways the following people were instrumental in making this book come to life. My warmest appreciation to:

William Agee
Dag Sebastian Ahlander and
    Gunilla von Arbin
Brigitta Almstrom
Ulrika Bengtsson
Lisa Björklund
Britt Blomqvist
Görel Bogärde
Charlotte Bonnier
Daniel and Marie-Louise Bonnier
Gaga Bonnier
Louise Carling
Jonas Carlsson
Jacob Cronstedt
Dick and Estelle deJounge
Pamela Diaconis
Ralph and Katarina Edenheim

Eric Fritzel
Carl and Jane Gezelius
Gunnel Gustafson
Elisabeth Halvarsson-Stapen
Annika Hanas
Christer Larsson
Lauren and Manaume Leksell
Eva Lewenhaupt
Fred and Stella Lindblad
Åke Livstedt
Egil Malmsten
Gisela Montan
Marianne Nilsson
Linda Nordberg
Leif Östman
Ulf Persson
Paige Peterson

Lena Rahoult
Anika Reuterswärd
Lena Rydin
Lars and Ursula Sjöberg
Marie Söderberg
Elsa and Walter Stackelberg
Margareta and Bo Stromstedt
Lovisa Tenglin
Margareta Valentin
Margaret von Platen
Margaretha Vreisen
Ann Wall
Babbi Wallenberg
Kristina Wängberg-Eriksson
Jane Wehtje
Jan and Peder Wendt
Hans Yngve and Anna Nyberg

And finally, I would like to acknowledge the help of the *Bringing It Home—Sweden* team: Ivan Terestchenko, a photographer and illustrator par excellence. Bo Niles, a gifted expert on architecture and decoration. Annetta Hanna, a patient and wonderful editor. The very talented doyennes of design, Donna Agajanian, Jane Treuhaft, and Clarkson Potter's Art Director, Robbin Gourley. Lauren Shakely, Clarkson Potter's Editorial Director, and Chip Gibson, the President of Crown Publishing, the guiding forces behind the Bringing It Home® series. And finally to my agent, Jeff Stone, my unwavering pillar of support.

CONTENTS

The common threads that unite all Swedish interiors: beautiful woods, soft muted colors, pure lines, and a delightful sense of light and space.

Ideas for your living room floors, walls, windows. What to know about selecting furnishings and fabrics. Plus, a guide to Gustavian style.

Sinking into a dreamy featherbed, and what you should know about goose down. Color washing the bedroom walls. The story of Carl Larsson.

INTRODUCTION

On the first day of summer in 1989 I became forever enchanted by the grace and beauty of Sweden. It was the fourth day of my trip—the first I had ever made to this pristine northern corner of Europe. After three days in Stockholm, a city so stunning it is often called "The Venice of the North," I was spending the day with Swedish friends in the archipelago, a network of islands fanning out from Stockholm into the Baltic Sea. By boat, we skipped along a stretch of sparkling blue water, flanked on either side by picturesque tree-tufted islands. Arriving at the cottage of a mutual friend, we eased the boat into the slip, hopped onto the dock, and strolled up to meet the rest of the family and see the house.

Actually, it wasn't "a" house at all, but rather a cluster of tidy red wooden structures, all impeccably designed and maintained: a smokehouse, for the fish caught on the island (some of the catch was kept fresh in a wire basket suspended under the dock); a sauna; a boathouse; a small cabin where the college-aged children could have their "space"; and the main house, a cottage brimming with charm.

We chatted on the sun-splashed deck outside the cottage overlooking the water, enjoying a drink and some delicious smoked salmon hors d'oeuvres. I was struck by how exquisite yet completely unpretentious the setting was. It seemed to simultaneously fulfill the dreams of the nature lover, the gourmet, and the connoisseur of good design. In that moment I realized that the Swedes— against all odds in our modern, high-tech culture—enjoy a very high standard of living while resisting the temptations of excessive consumption and ostentation. Their world is one of quiet beauty, where the soft pulse of Lutheran values —hard work, humility, and community responsibility—marries with an innate artistic sensibility and a deep appreciation for the land.

Like many Americans making their first trip to Sweden, I wondered why I had never heard much about this remarkable place. It is the fourth largest country in Europe, offering every possible modern convenience, a superb highway and transportation system, and city waters so clean you can fish and swim in them. Best of all, Sweden is blissfully uncrowded: fully 50 percent of the land is blanketed by forests and more than 90,000 lakes dot the landscape. The Swedes themselves are friendly but never forward. Almost everyone speaks English, and a large number claim fluency in three languages or more.

What the Swedes don't do well, however, is boast. Perhaps this is why it took so many years of European travel before I discovered the delicate Scandinavian beauty that so captivated me. What took no time at all, in contrast, was my decision to focus on Sweden as the third book in my *Bringing It Home* series.

Bringing It Home grew out of personal experience. For several years as the associate publisher of *Esquire* magazine, I traveled four or five times a year to our offices in London, Paris, and Milan to work with my colleagues. While I was not discontented with my own American culture, I must admit that I had an intensely positive reaction to the texture of life in Europe. The look, the feel, the sounds, and the scents gave me a profound sense of well-being. So much so that the first few days following each return were always marked by a yearning for what I had left behind.

Late in 1991 I left *Esquire* and began a new career as a freelance writer. An assignment in the fall of 1992 took me back to Europe. One day, an intriguing question came to mind: Is it possible to bring a country home? If I made a careful study of a particular lifestyle, could I identify its key elements—and then reassemble them back home in the United States?

Invigorated by the possibilities, I embarked on this series of books, allowing my heart to lead me back to the countries I loved. I made arrangements to spend extended periods of time with many different families. I became a sponge, soaking up every detail of daily life: how the table was set, how the beds were made, how to prepare favorite foods. I discovered that—just like God, it is said—European life is in the details. I realized that it was indeed possible to re-create the essence of what nourished me during my many visits to Europe.

Like all the books in the series, *Bringing It Home—Sweden* does not assume you have devoted years of your life to the study of interior design or haute cuisine. I focus instead on the more immediate questions: Why do Swedish houses feel so fresh and light? Why do the painted finishes look so rich and pearly? What is the secret to their perfectly poached salmon? We'll walk through Swedish homes, see how the Swedes live, and listen to their voices. Room by room, we'll observe how the Swedes create the environments they cherish, why they spend their time as they do, and what values they hold closest to their hearts. And through these images, you'll learn how to re-create in your own home the aspects of Swedish life that most appeal to you.

OPPOSITE: Swedish artisans have excelled for centuries in carved ornamentation. These antique doors display particularly handsome examples of channel grooves and floral decoration.

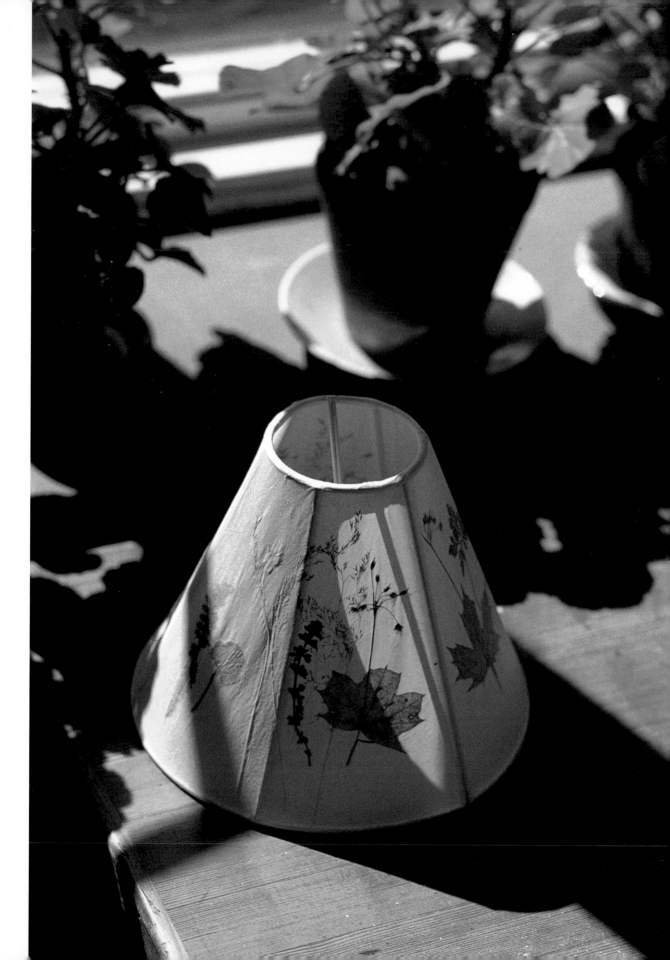

How to **Use** This **Book**

If someone asked you to describe yourself in a paragraph or two, you might make some generalizations that, although true, did not quite represent the full range of your character. You have many moods, many talents, many ways in which to express yourself.

Similarly, it is a challenge to describe the lifestyle of a country in one volume. Sweden has a sophisticated and complex culture that, despite a relatively small population (fewer than 9 million), has given rise to an amazing diversity of scientists, inventors, and artists, Alfred Nobel, Anders Zorn, Ingmar Bergman, and Greta Garbo being just four examples. Geographically, Sweden stretches over 15 degrees of latitude: from Lapland, which crosses the Arctic Circle, and where the sun shines continuously from May 29 to July 24, southward to the port city of Malmö, which almost kisses the coast of Denmark, Germany, and Poland. This elongated nation thus embraces a wide range in climate and landscape.

Aesthetically, Sweden is renowned for its blond woods and delicate color palette, yet the boldly colored folk art of Dalarna is also revered as a national treasure. There is much diversity in Sweden, and writers before me have very ably explored many of these intriguing areas in depth. (See Sources for some valuable books on Swedish culture.) I have instead chosen to focus on the common threads that unite the various regions and styles of Sweden. Above all, I am limiting these pages to those elements of life in Sweden that are most transportable—those elements that, in effect, define the difference between incorporating aspects of another culture into our lives and the mistaken belief that it is possible to "assume" another culture.

Bringing It Home—Sweden is constructed like a house. After a brief overview of the qualities that give a Swedish home its graceful appeal, the book is sectioned into rooms, beginning with the living room, where we look at the physical characteristics as they appear in both traditional and contemporary interiors. Where such aspects overlap—the way a window is dressed, for example—the subject is treated only once. And, beyond the physical appearance of a room, we'll examine the way life is lived within its walls: how guests are entertained or how meals are prepared, for example.

Equally important to re-creating the subtle beauty of Sweden in your own home is understanding the values and priorities of the Swedes themselves. To do so, I bring you the personal stories of artists and artisans whose sensibilities, attitudes, and convictions have shaped and will continue to shape the look and feel of Swedish life.

Bringing It Home—Sweden is, very simply, a guide to a lifestyle that embraces the benefits of the modern world, without forgoing an appreciation for beauty as defined by nature and tradition. In no way does it impose a rigid set of rules. Re-create whatever strikes your fancy. Pick and choose according to your own tastes and desires. And may you be as enchanted as I was that first day of summer in 1989.

OPPOSITE: The splendors of nature are beautifully showcased in Swedish designs. This parchment lampshade is one of a series created by the late Carl Malmsten. It remains in production today.

NATURAL
GRACE

TO ENTER A SWEDISH HOME is to be surrounded by a pure and delicate beauty, one that draws its inspiration from the graceful forms of nature. And like the slender white birch trees that rise from Sweden's landscape or the crystalline waters that bathe her shores, Swedish style recalls the exquisite freshness of a spring breeze.

By focusing on five characteristics—a devotion to wood, a reverence for light, a preference for muted tones, an apprecia-

Architect Jacob Cronstedt sought to bring his seaside home into harmony with its surroundings. Expansive views were cleverly designed for each room.

tion for fine lines, and an inclination to sparely furnished rooms—you will hold the keys to re-creating this sophisticated style in your own home.

A Glorious Profusion of WOODS

The lush forests that blanket 50 percent of Sweden's landscape have been graciously and imaginatively transplanted by its inhabitants into their homes for countless generations. Because it is so plentiful a resource, wood, primarily pine, ash, and birch, is the material of choice for every conceivable phase of home building and furnishing. Wood yields the frame, the walls, the floors, and the roof of a house, as well as the furniture and many of its accessories. It is planed, sanded, carved, stained, painted, and bleached. It is sliced, plaited, turned, and shaped into shelves, baskets, pegs, candleholders, boxes, toys, and even butter knives. In Sweden, wood and the interior are as inseparable as waves and the ocean.

Wood offers a particularly appealing feature to many Swedes: it is a democratic material. With its ready availability and reasonable cost, no one is excluded from trying his or her hand at fashioning something for the house—if not the house

Lightly stained or whitewashed wood appealingly evoke the charm of a Swedish country home. OVERLEAF: Peder Wendt's selection of antique doors, wide plank flooring, and an old gateleg table imbue his pavilion with timeless grace.

Everywhere in the Swedish home, wood makes its presence felt. Carved and painted Dalna horses are a favorite decorative object. Latches and handles are often crafted in wood. Max and Alexandra Bonnier play in the family's wood-sheathed sauna.

To enhance the presence of wood in your home, don't overlook the many small and useful objects such as bread boxes, peg racks for stemware or dishes, candlesticks, spice cabinets, or letter files that are created from this sympathetic and accommodating material.

The legendary Swedish furniture designer Carl Malmsten created this stunning design for a sewing table in the 1950s. The combination of delicate blond woods gives the piece an ethereal beauty. INSET: The Lewenhaupt family wanted a clean, modern look for their Stockholm apartment. Architect Jonas Bolin achieved the desired look with a liberal use of birch in combination with crisp stripes.

accent to her landscape. In the early 19th century, this honey blond wood also inspired Swedish cabinetmakers to craft their own interpretations of the somewhat heavier and darker Biedermeier-style furnishings coming from Germany. Their pale, sublimely beautiful creations came to be named the "Carl Johan style" (also known as "Swedish Biedermeier") for the Swedish monarch who reigned at the time.

While many of us reflexively conjure up visions of painted furniture when we think of Scandinavia and Sweden in particular, blond woods have enjoyed a long history in Swedish design. In 1939, Estrid Ericson, the founder of Svenskt Tenn, the illustrious home furnishings store that still does business from its fashionable location near the Royal Opera House in Stockholm, went so far as to say that wood "must not be painted or stained because it will immediately lose its charm and in fact be reduced to insignificance."

The leaders of the Swedish Modern movement that flourished during the 1940s, such as Ericson's partner Josef Frank (see page 136) and virtuoso cabinetmaker Carl Malmsten, also created a number of pieces from these light woods that still look fresh today. And Sweden's new generation of architects and designers continue to work almost exclusively in blond woods.

An undeniable purity can be conferred upon your rooms by furnishing them solely with pale, warm woods. The tone can be elegant and polished; imagine a Swedish Biedermeier sofa upholstered in

itself. While there are certainly a large number of woodworkers in Sweden who have achieved a high level of virtuosity in their chosen craft, almost every family member feels confident enough in his or her own skills to repair a chair, make a shelf, or construct a simple storage chest. Such is the strong preference for the look and feel of wood that even the dishwashers and refrigerators in many Swedish kitchens employ a wooden panel to camouflage the unwelcome appearance of metal doors.

NATURAL BLONDS

Like graceful ballerinas arching heavenward, the slender white birch trees that dapple Sweden's forests lend a delicate

WHEN BLOND WOODS SUCH AS BIRCH, PEAR, PINE, MAPLE, LEMON, AND SYCAMORE ARE EXPOSED TO THE ULTRAVIOLET RAYS OF SUNLIGHT, THEY CAN DISCOLOR AND TURN YELLOW— EVEN WHEN PROTECTED BY VARNISH. IF THE PROBLEM IS SEVERE, YOU SHOULD TURN TO A PROFESSIONAL WHO WILL BE ABLE TO RESTORE THE WOOD TO ITS ORIGINAL STATE BY STRIPPING IT. IF THE PROBLEM IS LESS SEVERE, YOU CAN CLEAN THE WOOD WITH A FINE-GRADE STEEL WOOL SUCH AS .00 GRADE AND THEN APPLY A LAYER OR TWO OF A NONTOXIC WATERBORNE POLYURETHANE, AVAILABLE AT HOME IMPROVEMENT STORES.

LEFT: To maximize the feeling of light and air, designer Louise Carling paired pine floors with white walls and ceilings. ABOVE: A milky purity was conferred to this kitchen counter by rubbing a small amount of whiting into the pine.

a white-on-white striped damask. Or it can be quite relaxed; consider an all-wood country kitchen outfitted with simple cabinets as well as a sturdy table and rush-seated chairs manufactured from white pine. Either way, the clean, soft tonality of light-colored wood will provide your home with a sense of freshness and clarity that makes for a thoroughly agreeable atmosphere.

A Thousand Points of Light

Midway through a Stockholm winter the sun rises at 8:47 A.M. and sets a scant six hours later at 2:45 P.M. Is it any wonder that the Swedes have consciously—and subconsciously—done everything possible to increase the amount of light in their homes and lives?

Even though the sun may linger a bit longer over your neighborhood, you can select from an impressive array of Swedish techniques to evoke a light and airy freshness any time of year. Windows, for example, are left undraped or, if privacy is an issue, dressed with just a touch of translucent voile.

Surfaces reflect light by virtue of being painted a light color or by being constructed from smooth blond woods. Fabrics are as pale of hue as the paint; if they sport a printed motif, it is set against a white background. Thickly textured and dark-toned fabrics that might display a tendency to absorb light are rarely if ever seen. Lamps and candles dot the rooms, with mirrors and glass objects generously placed to reflect their glow and enhance the effect of their light.

The Swedes have taken a formidable challenge from nature and triumphed in a brilliant show of light. The Swedes, in fact, understand a universal truth: no matter where we live, our spirits and moods are made much brighter by the presence of light.

Faceted glass transforms candle flames into a constellation of light that delights the senses.

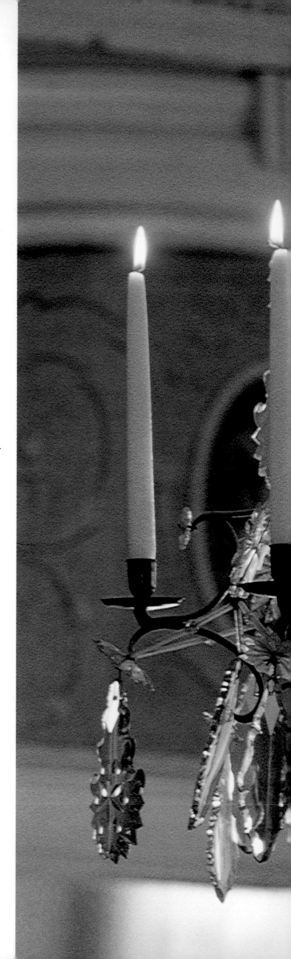

Myriad techniques can
be employed to bring
more light into an interior.
Gisela Montan uses only
light-colored fabrics and
paint and keeps a liberal
supply of candles about in
her Stockholm apartment.
ABOVE: A clear vase
amplifies the sunlight.

A LIGHTER
SHADE OF PALE

Since they are so sensitive to their environment, it comes as no surprise that many Swedes model their color combinations after the palettes composed by Mother Nature herself. Imagine dusk on the shores of one of the islands that form the archipelago fanning out from the city of Stockholm. The eye is met by endless, subtly changing layers of color: the sky is striated with delicate blues that subside into a diaphanous pink just at the surface of the sea, itself a symphony of gray-blues and gray-greens. The smooth rocks that meet the tide reveal yet another layer, one of chisel gray. For each shift in landscape, from fields of rolling flax to forests of rounded conifers, Sweden's landscape offers up an exquisite marriage of gently modulating colors—subtle, soft, and exceedingly refined.

In their interiors, the Swedes have become masters at nuance, playing one delicate hue off another. Recalling the metaphor of the onion, colors seem always able to reveal yet one more layer, a paler shade of blue, for example, or of straw or wheat. This art of variation is played out in fabrics as well as in the painted decoration of floors, walls, and furnishings.

Just the slightest hint of color can yield a dramatic effect. Note how the palest blues and grays soften this linen closet and the reading nook. OPPOSITE: Painter Hans Yngve created a welcoming environment by using this whisper-soft blue.

Covering the furnishings with pencil-striped cotton enhances the sense of refinement in this Gustavian room. LEFT: Narrow channel grooves carved into the doors and drawers of this console give it a clean, crisp character. The contemporary art of LG Lundgren displayed above is perfectly complemented by the antique piece.

FINE LINES

Throughout late 18th-century Europe, the playfully scrolling lines of the Rococo style gave way to the disciplined silhouette and straight lines of the Neoclassical style. The gently curved cabriole leg, for example, was replaced by the slim, channeled leg. Indeed, emphasizing the linearity of an object by carving a parallel series of fine vertical grooves was a favorite device of the epoch, and nowhere was it more enthusiastically embraced than in Sweden. Door panels, headboards and footboards, mirror frames, sideboards—any flat surface was a candidate for the woodworker's carving tools.

The Swedish love of the vertical, however, did not fade with the passing of Neoclassicism at the end of the 18th century in favor of the Biedermeier style. In fact, Sweden may be the most vertically oriented country in the world! Everywhere the eye roams, one cannot help but notice that contours tend to run up and down. On most Swedish exteriors, for example, wood siding is installed vertically and wood battens sheathe each seam—ostensibly to prevent water from seeping into any cracks, but more likely because the Swedes just love the uplifting silhouette it gives the house—to say nothing of the juxtaposition of the picket fences that set off the yard.

Inside the house, wooden interior paneling is also oriented vertically and grooved bevels, which serve to enhance the linear feeling, are considered a desirable extra touch. Even when it comes to

OPPOSITE: A pleasing and uplifting effect is created on an exterior by running the wood siding vertically and then applying wood battens to cover each seam. ABOVE: Channel grooves can be used with equal success in rustic or elegant settings. These exquisite footstools await placement in a newly renovated living room.

To bring the Swedish love of light and space into your home, choose furnishings with slender, tapered arms and legs. Occasional chairs might have wooden slat backs. Large pieces like chests, armoires, and sofas should have legs that allow you to see underneath. In the same spirit, avoid excessive draping of tables or upholstered seating with skirts.

soft furnishings, the Swedes can't get enough of their fine lines. Striped fabrics are enormously popular for upholstery, draperies, and bedding. And naturally enough, stripes are the pattern of choice for most of the rag runners that protect the wooden floors, themselves running in long straight planks.

CLUTTER-FREE ZONES

"A flat must be sparsely furnished . . . large heavy items of furniture should be avoided. . . . Never forget that one needs free floor space to move about." When Estrid Ericson committed her thoughts to paper in the first part of this century, she was not only articulating her own sense of style, but also making an observation of what had always worked in the finest Swedish interiors. Her partner Josef Frank went even further. In his 1934 essay entitled "Rooms and Furnishing," he wrote: "To have a pleasant effect, the room must be distinctly perceived. That is, all its boundary lines (in the ordinary prismatic room there are 12 of these altogether) and the surfaces indicating the size of the room (i.e., the ceiling and floor) must be visible entirely or without significant interruptions. [Thus] the furniture has to stand on feet which are high enough for the borderline between wall and floor to be visible (or at least discernible) underneath them. A box resting

The peaceful, airy tone of Linda Nordberg's New York dining room comes in large part from the tasteful restraint exercised in the furnishings. All pieces have slim silhouettes and no unnecessary elements clutter the room.

on its bottom surface destroys the borderline and floor space and with it every spatial effect." He further elaborates: "A chair with a solid backrest destroys the room because it conceals, whereas a Windsor-style back can be seen through."

The insights of Ericson and Frank notwithstanding, the need to perceive the boundaries of the room and the desire for floor space may be just part of the reason why most Swedish homes appear free of any clutter. Logically, in a land where light is revered, one would not long be able to tolerate heavy, clunky objects. (In fact, the few phases when Swedish interiors leaned toward the more robust preferences of their German neighbors passed very quickly.) Another factor is one of resources. Sweden has not been a particularly wealthy country throughout much of its history. In many households, the money simply did not exist for stocking up furnishings and objects that might make a visitor gasp for air or reel from ostentatious·display. Whether by need or preference, whether in Gustavian style or Modern, the Swedes create homes that are delicate, spare, and furnished with a down-to-earth elegance.

Designer Anika Reuterswärd has been called the Josef Frank of her generation. In her seaside dining room she mirrors Frank's belief that open backrests are preferable because they allow the eye and the light to pass freely through the room.

THE
LIVING
ROOM

NEARLY A CENTURY AGO, ARTIST Carl Larsson captured on his canvas all that is wonderful about a Swedish living room. It was a most enchanting scene: his young daughter Kersti waters the plants in the family living room while a soft light washes gently over the painted white windowsill and onto a wooden table where someone has been knitting. The room glows with a congenial warmth, and eloquently communicates its capacity

Carl Larsson began painting images of his children and home at the suggestion of his wife, Karin. His daughter Kersti is lovingly depicted in their living room.

Wide plank wooden
floors laid in a simple
end-to-end pattern
are a traditional style
in Sweden. Here the
look has been updated
with a high-gloss
urethane finish.

to welcome and shelter one and all.

The living room is the social center of home life in Sweden. It is where cups of strong coffee and delicious gingersnap cookies are enjoyed, where neighbors gather to share stories and families savor their leisure hours. To foster a sense of happiness and lighthearted well-being in the living room, especially during the winter months when the sun makes its all too brief daily appearance, the Swedes take myriad measures to ensure the perception of space and light within.

FLOORS IN FULL VIEW

Imagine strolling through a great manor house in Sweden. As you pass from the spacious drawing room into the elegant dining room, and on into the peacefully sophisticated bedrooms or even into the homely kitchen, one sound will follow you everywhere—the clicking of your heels on the silvery wooden floor planks.

From the most humble tradesman's cottage to the royal comforts of the king's palace, Swedish householders have steadfastly adhered to their preference for wooden floors. Uncovered and usually unpainted, these floors have weathered generations if not centuries of use, protecting feet against the cold, providing a solid and unifying platform for the room's furnishings, and growing more richly beautiful with each passing year.

Depending upon the wealth of the home owner and the era in which the floor was installed, variations are evident in how the wood was milled and laid, and how the floor was designed. Any of these variations will serve as a fine model for re-creating an authentic Swedish floor.

In the 17th and 18th centuries, when old-growth pine still forested much of Sweden, trees with massive trunks were readily available for harvest. Floors were laid with extremely wide planks, many a good 15 to 18 inches across. In more affluent houses, the boards (occasionally of more costly oak instead of pine) often were laid to imitate the parquet floors seen in elegant French homes.

In the average home, the simple end-to-end alignment of boards running parallel to the long walls of the room prevailed. These floors were protected by a thin coating of linseed oil, with perhaps a little whiting rubbed in to help lighten the atmosphere of the room. While other fashions have come and gone in the intervening years, this type of floor remains a true icon of Swedish interiors.

By the beginning of the 19th century, when slender second- or later-growth trees were replacing robust virgin forests, floorboards began to narrow. In finer houses, one also would note the use of slightly darker stains and a preference for the intricate types of parquet work being commissioned for the grand interiors of the French Empire of Napoleon Bonaparte's reign. In the 20th century, floors in many contemporary houses have been constructed with 3-inch-wide boards like the ones seen so often in the United States; those who place themselves on the cutting edge of design in

BLEACHING YOUR **FLOOR**

As an alternative to painting, consider bleaching your wooden floors to lighten them. Stockholm-based decorative painter Hans Yngve shared his technique with me.

1. Sand floors following the grain of the wood, using medium-grain sandpaper, #0. Rent a sanding machine for this task.

2. Apply a thin coat of calcium liquid bleach with a 4-inch-wide paintbrush, following the grain of the wood.

Allow to dry. Note: the first coat will leave the wood looking splotchy.

3. With the same-gauge sandpaper, sand the wood a second time.

4. Apply a second thin coat of bleach. Allow to dry.

5. Sand again with a very fine-grain sandpaper (.00).

6. Mix a small amount of whiting into boiled linseed oil. Both are available at home improvement stores and art stores. The ratio Hans likes best is two

tablespoons of whiting to one pint of boiled linseed oil; this amount will cover about 120 square feet. With a soft cloth, rub this into the surface of the wood. Vary the amount of whiting according to your tastes: if you prefer a paler look, sprinkle a little more whiting into the oil. Allow to dry thoroughly.

7. Change the sanding attachment to the softest buffer attachment and polish the floor.

Sweden now install such floors in white oak or bleached pine.

To install a plank floor, there are practical as well as aesthetic considerations to take into account. A 3-inch-wide plank (which narrows to about 2½ inches when prepared by the mill for its tongue-in-groove installation) is the most resistant to warping from fluctuations in heat and humidity. Wider planks more authentically represent the traditional Swedish style but, unless nailed through the top to the subfloor, will tend to buckle slightly during normal changes in weather. These small undulations, however, are viewed by many people as pleasing.

Many Swedish floors are painted in simple motifs, rooted in the country's folk art traditions. Re-creating motifs such as large diamonds rendered in quintessentially pale Scandinavian hues is a wonderful way to evoke a Swedish ambiance. Stencils, too, scattered over the field of a floor or accenting its border, can be created with basic painting skills.

To capture the luminous beauty of Swedish painted floors, be sure to avoid a chalky, opaque surface. The objective is to provide color and pattern without obliterating the feeling of the wood underneath. (Interestingly, in Swedish, the words for "wood" and "tree" are very close—perhaps indicative of the desire that the character of a tree never get lost in the use of its wood.) Although more time-consuming, Swedish home owners will apply many thin, almost translucent layers of paint rather than one or two viscous coats.

Bleached floorboards confer a gentle warmth to a room and work well with traditional or contemporary furnishings.

DIAMONDS **UNDERFOOT**
FOUR EASY STEPS TO A CLASSIC SWEDISH FLOOR

Painting your floor in a diamond motif is a charming way to evoke the atmosphere of a Swedish home. With a weekend to spare and a minimum of painting skills, anyone can achieve a satisfying result.

First, select a pair of compatible colors. For an authentic Swedish-style floor, choose from nature's palette. Avoid too strong a contrast between your hues; combinations like pale gray and gray-blue, or cream and celadon, look best together (see color palette, page 177). The Swedes traditionally work with tempera paints (see page 176), which are not well known in the United States; these are paints mixed from linseed oil, powdered pigments, and mineral spirits. In my own home, I have used water-soluble latex porch/floor paint from Dutch Boy for diamond-motif floor patterns and found the results quite satisfactory. Latex paints are easy to work with because they go on smoothly, dry quickly, and are easy to clean up after, although, of course, some of the special character offered by tempera paints is lost.

Second, make sure the floor is clean and prepared for painting. Floors that are waxed, varnished, or polyurethaned will need to be sanded down to bare wood, or primed, or both.

Third, prepare the ground color for your

diamonds. Using a 4-inch-wide bristle brush, paint the entire floor with two coats of your lighter color, making sure to follow the grain of the wood. It is well worth investing in a good-quality brush since inexpensive brushes shed bristles into your wet paint, and do not give a good, smooth finish. Allow to dry completely, according to the manufacturer's directions, between the two coats. Sand lightly between coats to prevent peeling or flaking.

Fourth, when the floor is thoroughly dry, you can begin to create your grid of diamonds. I find it helpful to draw the room to scale on paper before making any marks on the floor. Use graph paper with four squares to an inch; let two squares, equal to $1/2$ inch, represent 1 foot. Experiment by drawing diamonds on paper until the number of diamonds and their proportions are agreeable to you. Then, bumping up the scale from the graph to the actual floor size, you can figure out the distance between the points of the diamonds that you will mark around the periphery of the floor.

It can be difficult to gauge a diamond pattern so that it fits precisely within the boundaries defined by the walls, especially if the wall is punctuated by jogs or built-ins, such as a hearth. In many American homes, the diamonds will necessarily "bleed" into the walls. If you want to fol-

low this format, you should position one diamond in the exact center of the room so that a row of diamonds runs down the middle of the room, in both directions. This way, once all the diamonds are painted on the floor, the room will not appear to "veer off" in one direction or the other.

Painting the Diamonds

Step 1. Because most floors comprise a large surface, marking will go faster if you work with a partner. With a steel tape, measure the length and width of your room. For the purpose of this illustration, let's say the floor is 12 feet by 10 feet. In a room this size I would place 4 diamonds across and 4 diamonds lengthwise; these proportions felt right to me, but again, experiment on your graph paper to see what works best for your own space.

Step 2. Divide the length and the width of the room by 8 (double the number of diamonds in our hypothetical room). Twelve feet breaks into eight 18-inch sections; 10 feet, into eight 15-inch sections. Make a small mark in pencil every 18 inches at the edge of the floor along both long walls; repeat this procedure every 15 inches, across the two short walls.

Step 3. Using a chalk line (available in any home improvement store), you and your partner should start in one corner of the room and locate the first mark out from the corner in each direction. Snap the chalk line to connect. Move to the third mark out and repeat. Continue to connect every other mark, until the entire room is marked out in parallel lines. Then repeat this process in the other direction to make a second set of parallel lines that intersects your first set.

Step 4. The chalk marks on your floor will define the outlines of your diamonds. With painter's tape or 1-inch-wide heavy-duty masking tape, tape off the outlines of the diamonds to be painted. Press the tape firmly, so that no paint can bleed under the edges. (Run the wooden edge of a small paintbrush along the edge.) Using a 4-inch-wide bristle brush, work with the direction of the grain and apply two coats of the darker paint to the inside of the diamonds. Allow to dry thoroughly between coats and after. Remove the tape.

If you like the idea of your floor's attaining a weathered look, leave the paint alone so that scuff marks will build up over time. If you defer to practicality, you can seal your handiwork with two coats of a matte-finish, waterborne polyurethane. Following the manufacturer's instructions, apply one coat, allow to dry thoroughly, then brush on the second coat.

Floor Coverings with Charm

During the 18th century, upper-class families in Europe had begun to enjoy the availability of finely woven cut-pile carpets that were being manufactured in England. Those of moderate or lower incomes, on the other hand, found their floor coverings in an ingenious new method some English companies had developed of weaving cloth strips together. These "listed carpets," as they were called, were flat runner-type rugs that could be sewn together to make larger floor coverings.

Sweden at this time was still feeling the economic stress of a prolonged war with Russia and its aftermath. Listed carpets were thus the only affordable option for imported floor coverings, even among the upper classes. Instead of sewing the individual carpets together, however, wealthy Swedes tended to use them as runners to protect high-traffic areas. With the example of their upper-class neighbors in mind, Swedish families of more modest means made similar runners on home looms. To do so, they saved scraps of cloth, tore these rags into narrow strips, and wove them through a warp of coarse linen thread. By sorting the colors of the rags used during the weaving process, pleasing stripes and variations in colors could be achieved.

It was not merely economic stresses, however, that led to the prevalence of the rag runner; it was Swedish preferences, too. The Swedes perceive beauty in the simplest of things, be they natural or handcrafted, and they exhibit a pronounced practical streak. The rag runner perfectly embodies both traits, and so has endured as the floor covering of choice in many Swedish homes.

To use these charming striped runners as they are seen in traditionally decorated homes, place them along the periphery of the room, about 30 inches away from the wall. Chairs should be pushed up against the wall, behind the runner. When the runner approaches a corner, simply turn it over on itself, at a 90-degree angle, and let it continue in a perpendicular direction. Carl Larsson's delightful views of family life, painted in the early 1900s, show many variations on this placement of the runner.

Today, runners are ubiquitous in the Swedish kitchen. In the living room, rag rugs expand to greater proportions. A square or rectangular rug woven from cloth strips is used under the seating area in many homes.

As universally loved as the runner may be, it is not the only floor covering seen in Sweden. In traditionally decorated homes where the budget is more liberal, Oriental rugs have long been favored. In contemporary interiors, particularly among younger urban families, there is a preference for geometrically patterned pile rugs. Both types of rugs, in contrast to the runners used on the periphery of the room, are placed under the main seating area.

In the homestead of Carl Larsson, a classic blue and white carpet is placed over the scrubbed pine floors.

WALLS WITH CHARACTER

In Sweden, walls do not function merely to divide interior spaces or to support a ceiling. Walls are canvases for self-expression. For centuries, while their European neighbors to the south lavished their walls with tapestries, silks, and fine printed papers, the Swedes were imaginatively extending the boundaries of painted decoration.

Using their own homemade distemper paints, a combination of chalky pigments from the earth, linseed oil, and glue from animal skin, all manner of designs were being created. In finer homes one might see painters affix canvas to the wall and then experiment with Rococo motifs copied from French pattern books. In more modest homes, paint was applied to imitate expensive woods or porphyry, a feldspar-flecked stone found on outcroppings throughout Sweden. In the countryside, walls played host to colorful folkloric interpretations of myth and history.

While painting is a quintessentially Swedish way of decorating the wall, the Swedes have also created many fine wallpapers, and, of course, wooden paneling is used extensively in many homes. Over the next few pages we'll look at a range of wall treatments, paying particular attention to the painting techniques that can easily be duplicated in any home.

Motifs based on floral designs rendered in the blues and grays of the Scandinavian palette are a classic form of wall decoration in Sweden.

THE ART OF PAINTING

If an Aubusson tapestry or Neoclassical paneling don't quite fit into your budget, there is no need to remove them entirely from your decorating plans. Swedish painters have been brilliantly imitating these and countless other wall decorations for centuries.

A particular fondness for partitioning walls into "frames" and "panels" tops the list of preferred painting techniques. In traditionally decorated homes, Swedish painters use two techniques that originated in the Italian Renaissance. The first, trompe l'oeil, realistically renders actual subjects, such as scenic landscapes, in order to "trick the eye"; the second, grissaille, is a method whereby the subject, often stone or statuary, is mimicked in shadings of gray.

Whereas the wall panels on the European continent typically contained silks, tapestries, or fine oil paintings in gilded frames, their Swedish counterparts were not panels at all, but simply pieces of linen canvas stretched and painted to resemble paneling. The open fields defined by the "moldings" of these faux panels, executed in the soft color palette the Swedes love, never appear empty or incomplete. Instead, they give the room a delicious touch of sophistication and refinement, as if it were obvious that less would be more.

A most attractive quality of these painted panels is that, with a small invest-

RIGHT: Distemper paint has been used to yield the soft powdery blue on this wall. OPPOSITE: A classic Gustavian detail.

ment in materials and just a modicum of skills, we can add atmosphere to the unadorned rectangular living rooms common to so many modern homes. A number of informative books are available (see Sources) to guide you through the painting process; many are illustrated with photographs accompanied by step-by-step instructions.

A less stately, but equally charming, approach to partitioning and painting walls is to work with stencils; another is the technique known as spatter painting. In both treatments, the wall generally divides horizontally at the height of a chair rail. The lower portion of the wall typically is faux-painted to resemble speckled porphyry, or it is cloaked in a solid color. The upper portion is then spatter-painted in a second shade, or it is stenciled to resemble wallpaper.

Lastly, sponging or color washing walls are fine choices if you enjoy the art of illusion. When executed in the Swedish palette, these techniques impart a richness to the wall that is difficult to achieve with a single color. Like the other painting techniques mentioned here, they are fairly easily and quickly accomplished by the do-it-yourselfer. (See "Soft Palettes," page 92, and the box on page 81.)

Swedish artists have created breathtakingly beautiful designs in every epoch of the nation's history. CLOCKWISE FROM FAR LEFT: Late 18th-century Neoclassic motif; 17th century; again, late 18th-century Neoclassic; detail from Gustavian manor house; National Romantic period (about 1900).

HOW TO **TRANSFER** A MOTIF

Decorative artist Hans Yngve, based in Stockholm, is frequently called upon by clients to re-create the glorious Neoclassical motifs favored by King Gustav III. Although native talent and years of practice have made Hans one of the most accomplished in his field, he claims that the basic techniques used in his art can be practiced at home by any amateur. He used the following step-by-step technique to re-create a stunning motif in a stately home that had been damaged by fire.

1. Tracing paper was placed over a section of the motif not damaged by the fire and the lines of the design were traced in pencil. You can create similar tracings using pattern books, historical photographs enlarged to a size that suits your space, or any manageable image you can find.

2. The tracing paper is placed on top of several sheets of newspaper. With a spoked tracing wheel, small perforations in the tracing paper are made along the lines of the design.

3. The perforated tracing paper is positioned on the wall, and held in place with a bit of masking tape. A small square of cheesecloth is filled with about a tablespoon of powdered chalk, gathered up with an elastic to form a little pouch, and then tapped gently against the perforated tracing paper, making sure to completely cover the entire surface.

4. When the paper is removed, a series of dots describing the original pattern has been transferred to the wall. The dots are then connected lightly with a pencil.

5. Copying colors from the original work, the motif is repainted within the connect-the-dots outline.

THE WHITE WALL

"The modern living room has white walls," said Josef Frank in 1934. Frank was the talented architect/designer who, with Estrid Ericson, founded Stockholm's Svenskt Tenn home furnishings store, and who was one of the foremost proponents of the Swedish Modern movement. To home owners who wished to break free from the tradition of painted decorations or wallpapers that characterized homes of an earlier Sweden, Frank advised that pure white walls "were the only possible way of preserving one's liberty" in the living room. White walls, he continued, allowed one to "introduce whatever one likes without being distracted by the color decorations."

Frank's goal, and that of his fellow Modernists, was the freedom to use boldly hued fabrics in the living room without having to compete with the walls for attention. And this was not to be a passing style. Although the strict designs of the Modernists were never entirely to dominate Swedish interiors, they made lasting changes in the range of styles considered to be in good taste. For Swedes today who desire a fresh modern tone for their interiors, white walls are still de rigueur.

Believing that white walls allow for the most effective display of distinctly patterned fabrics, the late architect Josef Frank would have been delighted to see his sofa design for Svenskt Tenn in this Stockholm apartment.

PANELED WALLS

When architect Jacob Cronstedt (whose great-great-grandfather Carl Johan Cronstedt in 1767 invented the ceramic stove, an icon of the Swedish interior) built his new home in the Swedish archipelago, he crafted its interior entirely of wood. The house, which exhibits a remarkable quality of timelessness, looks as rooted in Sweden's rural past as it epitomizes the present. Much of the credit for this balancing act goes to the walls, which Cronstedt paneled in a rough-hewn pine lightly washed with whiting.

With both abundant timber resources and a love for the aesthetic qualities of wood, paneling has long been employed in Swedish homes. The first extensive use of paneling, dating back to the 18th century, was on the exteriors of houses. Once the house itself was framed with horizontally laid timbers, vertical planks and battens were attached as weatherproofing. In aristocratic dwellings, finely finished vertical boards or dadoes might then also be installed on the interior, in the "best rooms." Otherwise, the inside surfaces of the horizontally laid timbers were painted directly or covered with wallpaper.

In the 19th century, when milling technology advanced, the Swedes began to employ tongue-and-groove wainscoting or matchstick–effect paneling to cover all or part of the wall. Artist Carl Larsson's home in Sundborn (see page 100), which profoundly influenced the decoration of Swedish homes, displays particularly handsome wainscoting in some of its rooms.

WOOD PANELING IS A WONDERFUL CHOICE FOR BRINGING THE BEAUTY OF NATURE INTO YOUR LIVING ROOM. DEPENDING ON THE TYPE OF PANELING YOU CHOOSE, YOU CAN CREATE A NUMBER OF DIFFERENT MOODS. FOR RUSTIC CHARM, SELECT FLAT BOARDS THAT MEASURE AT LEAST 6 INCHES WIDE. BASED ON YOUR PREFERENCES, ASK THE LUMBERYARD FOR EITHER A SMOOTH OR A SLIGHTLY ROUGH-HEWN FINISH. (SOME BOARDS ARE MILLED WITH ONE SMOOTH SIDE AND ONE ROUGHER SIDE.) RUN THE PANELS FROM FLOOR TO CEILING, EITHER LEAVING THEM IN THEIR NATURAL STATE, PROTECTED WITH JUST A THIN COATING OF BOILED LINSEED OIL, OR APPLY A WHITE OR GRAY COLOR WASH. TO CREATE A HANDSOME ARTS AND CRAFTS–INSPIRED LOOK, OPT FOR A NARROWER BOARD (APPROXIMATELY 3 TO 4 INCHES WIDE) AND CONSIDER TONGUE-AND-GROOVE OR BEVELED EDGES TO EMPHASIZE THE PLEASING LINEARITY; AGAIN, YOU CAN PROTECT THE WOOD IN ITS NATURAL STATE WITH JUST A LITTLE BOILED LINSEED OIL, OR PAINT IT A PALE SCANDINAVIAN HUE.

OPPOSITE: To evoke a rustic feeling, consider wooden paneling painted in a soft hue like the yellow depicted in this water-color. LEFT: Rough-sawn wood paneling rubbed with zinc and titanium white gives a timeless and natural tone to the home of architect Jacob Cronstedt. In contrast to many Swedish homes, the paneling was installed horizontally.

CLASSIC WALLPAPERS

In Sweden, as in other European countries and the United States, early wallpapers were largely created to resemble textile patterns of the period. As tastes changed in fabric motifs, wallpaper designs followed suit. The Swedes have consistently preferred pale, airy designs for their papers, although at the turn of the century, British Arts and Crafts patterns inspired a series of jewel-toned naturalistic patterns.

Today's Swedish wallpapers bring a wonderfully fresh and sophisticated feeling to any room (see Sources). Not surprisingly, the most popular colors and motifs reflect the national preference for white or light-colored grounds, with fine, classic medallion-type patterns placed within an overall striped motif. For a crisp, contemporary look, a straightforward stripe is used, with no secondary pattern introduced. And a lovely option for those who treasure the gifts of the garden are papers printed with exquisite botanical drawings inspired by the work of Sweden's famous son Carl Linnaeus, the 18th-century botanist who revolutionized the field of classifying plant species.

LEFT: Anders and Veronica Öhman, like most Swedish couples, prefer a clean airy feeling in the home. Thus a light ground color and delicate design was selected for their wallpaper. FAR LEFT: Lotta Bonnier's teal- and white-striped paper is a perfect complement for the marine motif of her paintings.

ARRANGING THE
FURNITURE

When entering a Swedish living room, one might be excused for momentarily wondering whether the walls had exerted some magnetic force upon the furnishings, for it often appears as if almost every object in the room were drawn toward, if not literally glued to, the periphery of the room. In traditionally decorated homes, wooden-backed chairs line the walls like so many debutantes waiting for an invitation to dance. Sofas or settees and semicircular tables are similarly situated. Only the tea table and two or three visitor's chairs are placed out in the center of the room in front of the sofas, to create a congenial seating group.

This classic arrangement of furnishings is both pleasing and practical: the room not only feels wonderfully open and spacious, but offers great flexibility to accommodate all sorts of activities. Tables and chairs can be brought from the periphery to the center as needed; most of the time, however, the center of the room remains clear.

Like most Swedish aesthetic principles, the preferences for flexibility and open space trace their origins to the marriage of thrift and practicality with an innate sense of refinement. As in many countries, primitive Swedish dwellings

Flexibility is the key to Swedish furniture arrangements. Aside from one or two guest chairs that may face the sofa, other pieces are kept against the wall and brought out as needed.

comprised one large common room that had to serve a variety of purposes: cooking, dining, working, entertaining, even sleeping.

To make the most of this space, particularly during the lean periods of their history when little money was available for decorating a house, the Swedes combined their talent for woodworking with their mechanical skills to devise furnishings that performed double duty. Benches built in along the wall provided not only seating but storage. Wooden sofas pulled out to become beds. Dining tables folded up into sections and could be stored alongside the wall; when unfolded, they could be set end to end to compose one long table. Chairs were light and easily moved. Smaller occasional tables were often built with tilting tops so that they, too, could be tucked into a corner of the room when not called into service.

The brilliance of these 17th-century solutions is evident in their continuing appeal to today's families in Europe and America. Houses may now be larger, but our appetite for space seems never to be sated. An entry hall bench that will store shoes and umbrellas under a hinged seat, a console that opens to an extra dining table to accommodate holiday guests, or a collection of easily moved Gustavian-style chairs that allows a gathering of four to blossom into a gathering of eight, are just some examples of how our modern lives can be rendered more livable by the use of flexible furnishings.

In the 19th century, the look of Swedish living room furniture began to

change but the manner of arranging it stayed consistent with traditional desires for spacious living rooms. Fully upholstered sofas presented a more relaxed alternative to the wooden-backed models, but they were still generally pushed up against the wall, rather than set out in the middle of the floor to demarcate a conversational grouping or function as room dividers. In fact, the scale of furnishings even today conforms to architect/designer Josef Frank's advice from the early 1900s: "Small furniture makes the room big. . . . A piece of furniture should not be one single millimeter larger than its purpose requires, because this would be contrary to the basic aesthetic principle of economy."

Another way in which the Swedes continue to honor their traditional customs is through their arrangement of the seating group. Coffee tables, although not rare, are not as firmly entrenched as they are in American homes. A significant number of Swedish families prefer to use a tea table—which is approximately 28 inches high rather than the 16- to 18-inch height of the coffee table—placing it in front of the sofa and accompanying it with two armchairs.

The half-round table is a brilliant example of Swedish furnishing strategies. When not needed, it remains along the wall, functioning as a console. For entertaining, it can be reunited with its twin and brought to the center of the room for a full-size dining table.

When arranging the furniture in your living room, place larger pieces like sofas and loveseats back up against the walls. The center area of the room should be clear, or as sparsely furnished as possible; just a slender-legged tea table and a couple of light chairs or ottomans for additional seating should complete the setting.

SELECTING **A SOFA**

To create the graceful, airy feeling so characteristic of a Swedish living room, look for a sofa that meets a few basic criteria: the legs should be visible and slender; the back and arms should present a clean, distinct silhouette; the overall frame should never appear massive. Whether your tastes lean to city contemporary or country classic, a sofa with these qualities will impart a peaceful and elegant tone to your room.

Many classic Swedish sofas were designed with decoratively carved aprons. Here vertical grooves enhance the sofa's clean lines, but carved floral and strapwork motifs would work equally well to bring a classic 18th-century style to a room. Note that the wooden backboard and arm panels are fashioned at the same height.

This model is also a classic design, but key differences from the sofa above give it a lighter, more refined look. The absence of an apron, the band of open rails, the lightly upholstered back, the small-scale check motif, and the use of round bolsters instead of square pillows create a very light and graceful profile.

If a modern decor is desired, this sofa is an excellent choice. The young designer Thomas Sandell remained true to the traditional Swedish preference for impeccably clean silhouettes, yet with its fully upholstered frame and bold coloring, the model he created for IKEA PS is undeniably fresh (see Sources).

CLASSIC FABRICS

Natural fibers, and linen particularly, have long been favored in Sweden for their durability, softness, and inherent beauty. Swedish fabrics, whether finely woven table and bath linens, or more coarsely woven upholstery textiles, are expected to last for many generations. Until recently a large percentage of Swedish homes had looms, and even families of modest means would have up to several dozen tablecloths, towels, and sheets of handwoven linen.

Today Swedish weavers continue to produce some of the most beautiful linen, cotton, and cotten-linen fabrics to be found. Many are damask fabrics, such as the magnificent Klässbol cloths that grace the tables at the annual Nobel Awards banquet. Others feature stunningly handsome document prints dating back to the 18th century and engraved on copper plates. But perhaps the most charming of all are the fabrics confected with the simple manipulations of warp and weft threads that produce the classic stripes and checks.

Axel, Thor, and Emma play on pillows covered in a quintessential Swedish ticking stripe.

CHECKS AND STRIPES FOREVER

Classic Swedish fabrics belong to one of three families: stripes, checks, or motifs inspired by nature, particularly leaves and flowers. But while the categories may be few in number, the variations on the basic themes are infinite and delightful.

Stripes with their varied repetitions, widths, and colorways lend an appealing energy and crispness to a decor.

They can be successfully paired with checks, both large and small, and used in any room in the house. Botanical prints, classically executed on light backgrounds, impart a softer, more refined style and are an excellent choice for evoking the lightness and grace of the 18th century. All of the classic fabrics on these two pages are still in production. See page 178 for details.

"Medeviruta"/IKEA
18th Century

"Gripsholm Red"/
Svenskt Tenn

All fabrics from
"Bolster"/Lena Rahoult

"Gripsholm Blue"/
Svenskt Tenn

"Ekebyholm"/IKEA
18th Century

"Svaneholm"/
Country Swedish

"Ulrika"/IKEA
18th Century

"Elephant"/
Svenskt Tenn

"Ferns"/Sanderson

"Rosebud"/
Jobs-Royal Sweden

"US Tree"/
J. Frank-Svenskt Tenn

"Rose Trellis"/
Jobs-Royal Sweden

With the objective of maximizing the light entering a room, many Swedish windows are simply not draped. Others carry perhaps just a swag to soften their appearance. When a more formal style is desired, as in the drawing room of Nynas Manor (LEFT), long draperies composed of narrow panels are used.

WINDOWS

Just after the turn of the 20th century, a book of Swedish interiors painted by Carl Larsson was published in Germany with the title *Lasst Licht Hinein*, or *Let in More Light*. While the name was meant to describe interiors in general, it captures the essence of Swedish window dressing, where access to light, that precious commodity during the long Scandinavian winters, is all-important. Larsson and many other Swedish artists depict the window as an animator of family life; subjects holding needlework, books, or correspondence sit next to windows accented with the most diaphanous of cloths—perhaps just a swag across the top of the sash, or narrow panels falling gently to each side—so that the sunlight bathes the area around them.

Today the favored window dressing in Swedish living rooms seems to be no dressing at all. It is a delightfully pure and simple look, where the wooden window frames cleanly define the boundary between the interior and the scene that lies just outside. Every last ray of sunshine is welcomed into the room.

When some type of fabric is desired to soften the look, many Swedes turn to a swag or valence. The white muslin swag held by rosettes is an icon of the Neoclassical era and remains popular as Sweden heads into the 21st century. The swag itself can loop two or three times around the traverse rod; the tails generally hang a quarter to a third the length of the window. A straight valence provides more of an informal, country look. Again, the typical fabric choice is a white muslin, and the valence covers approximately the top quarter of the window.

Long curtains can be found throughout Sweden and are another option to create a Swedish ambiance in your living room. These are almost always composed of relatively narrow panels, however, which are then pulled well to the side of the window with a tieback. Curtains can be teamed with a swag or a valence, or they may hang in a straightforward manner from a traverse rod. Remember, the light must never be blocked from entering the room; heavy fabrics, therefore, would not be an appropriate choice.

To create a window dressing that beautifully captures the charm and sophistication of 18th-century Sweden, consider the cotton roller blind, fashioned in a softly hued check or striped fabric and used in combination with a swag or full drapes, or simply used alone. These clever mechanisms first appeared in Europe in the late 1600s. Unlike the spring-loaded rolling window shades or the venetian blinds seen so often in the United States, they consist of a wooden dowel cut to the width of the window, wrapped with fabric cut to the window's length, and rolled up and down by means of a cotton cord that loops the rolled fabric and runs up through a metal ring mounted on the window frame. During Sweden's summer months of near nonstop sunlight, these blinds nicely filter the strong light that might otherwise fade a room's furnishings.

ABOVE: Babbi Wallenberg has the good fortune to live by the sea. Her living room windows remain undraped to take full advantage of the views. OPPOSITE, TOP: Cotton roller blinds, operated by a simple pulley, are a traditional Swedish window treatment. OPPOSITE, BOTTOM: Long, diaphanous panels catch a soft breeze.

CELEBRATING
NATURE

The Swedes can fish and swim in the water flowing through the canals of Stockholm. How many capital cities of industrialized nations can make this claim?

In Sweden, nature is celebrated and protected. The Swedes believe their physical and emotional well-being is inextricably connected to the health of their environment. Their outlook resonates through the many layers of their lives. Take, for example, the national holiday celebrating the summer solstice, when every village constructs a tall maypole dressed with leaves and flowers. Consider also the colors they prefer for the decoration of their houses, such as the soft blue of the sky or the pearly gray of the smooth

rock that wraps Sweden's shoreline. And think of the great numbers of Swedes who catch and smoke their own fish, harvest berries in season to make preserves, and supplement their summer menus with vegetables grown in the garden.

In the decoration of the home, countless objects are brought directly from the outdoors and integrated into the tableau: seashells displayed in a basket, moss tucked around the base of a candle, supple vines woven into a wreath. Additionally, the natural forms serve as the inspiration for many ornaments in the home— carved decoys being a particular favorite.

In weaving the beauty of nature into your own home, look with fresh eyes at the landscape around you. Chances are there are many things you never considered closely that could embellish the decor of any room and inspire a feeling of well-being. Some easy projects to consider: Collect pinecones and pile them into interestingly shaped glass urns or cubes. Decorate a wooden picture frame by gluing small twigs or pieces of driftwood onto the surface in a free-form design. Use a slim branch in place of a traverse rod to hang a light muslin curtain. There is, indeed, no end to the imaginative ways we can weave nature's bounty into every room of our homes.

The Swedes are brilliant at weaving bits of the landscape into the interior. OPPOSITE: Objects from the sea decorate a desk. BELOW: Decades ago the late Carl Malmsten designed a series of lampshades featuring pressed leaves. They remain a top seller in the Stockholm store that bears his name. ABOVE: Curly twigs are fashioned into a nest in homage to the architectural ingenuity of feathered friends.

GUSTAV III

Only a very small number of people in history have held such impassioned convictions in aesthetic matters and exercised such force in dictating tastes that they have become eponymous with the style of their time. Gustav III, king of Sweden from 1771 until his death just twenty-one years later, is one such figure, and Gustavian style is arguably one of the most enlightened and refined in the pantheon of European decorative arts. Today, his stature grows as people rediscover that the classic purity he extolled creates interiors that are both sophisticated and serene.

Gustav was born in 1746 to Lovisa Ulrika of Prussia, the sister of Frederick the Great of Prussia, and Adolf Fredrick, King of Sweden, who reigned from 1751 to 1771. Thanks largely to the influence of his mother, whose friends included Voltaire and other French intellectuals, Gustav's early years were spent studying French culture and language. In fact it was during a trip to France that the 25-year-old crown prince was notified of his father's death and summoned back to Stockholm to assume the throne.

Young Gustav had ravenous appetites for beauty and knowledge as well as for power. His heroes were the French kings Henri IV and Louis XIV, and he imported the formal etiquette of Versailles to his court. He had a passion for theater and installed a full-sized private theater in the royal castle of Gripsholm, northwest of Stockholm. Gustav also collected detailed architectural drawings from the French court and other grand buildings in France from which he drew inspiration for the style he was to espouse.

As is often the case in eponymous styles, Gustav did not so much invent a style as display the skills of a brilliant editor or curator. He knew what talent to foster, which forms to accept and which to reject, and what objects to bring back from his trips abroad and what to leave behind.

Gustavian style, therefore, synthesizes three important developments the young royal observed in his European travels.

LEFT: A handsome bust of King Gustav III stands in Skogaholm Manor, located on the grounds of the Skansen open-air museum. RIGHT: The green drawing room in Nynas Manor exemplifies the refined aesthetics of the Gustavian era. Note the meticulously executed wall panels with their beautiful scrolling motifs.

First was a strong reaction against the Rococo style, which had grown excessive. Second, the discovery of the entombed cities of Herculaneum and Pompeii and the gradual availability of books documenting the Greco-Roman designs found at the excavations favored a taste for classical architecture. Third, the publication of Jean-François de Neufforge's influential *Recuil Élémentaire d'Architecture (Collection of Architectural Elements)*, between 1757 and 1770, offered an illustrated compendium of the ornamental motifs (laurel wreaths, garlands, medallions) that Gustav employed so prolifically in his commissioned designs.

On extended visits that Gustav took through France and Italy, he met and engaged the talents of highly skilled architects and craftsmen. The coordinated efforts of these artisans gave birth to a style that, while influenced by the Neoclassicism that flourished under France's Louis XVI, is distinguished by its uniquely Scandinavian color palette, its exquisite measures of lightness and purity, and its resistance to any ostentation. Gustavian style serves as a breathtaking reminder that no style is ever purely of one country or one period. Here, an aesthetic evolved that was executed by a European force of artisans directed by a Swedish monarch, who was enamored of the designs of a French court, which in turn was enthralled by the architectural precepts of ancient Greece.

Gustav's demise offers a certain ironic twist to the style he so ardently embraced, which rose to popularity as a reaction against excess and as a representation of purer values. Gustav himself was an insatiable despot whose relentless pursuit of power turned many against him. In 1792 he was assassinated while attending a masked ball in Stockholm.

This canopied bed is also in Skogaholm. The classical motifs carved into the footboard are typical of the epoch, as is the reddish-brown color often referred to as English red.

A QUICK GUIDE TO
GUSTAVIAN
STYLE

With roots in classical Greece, the hallmarks of Gustavian style are, above all, clean lines and symmetry. Rooms are well-proportioned and spare, almost austere in their relationship between space and furnishings. Floors are covered with planks of scrubbed pine, which give a uniform silvery gray cast to the room. Walls are visually divided into panels, with insets of canvas often decorated with classical motifs such as garlands, laurel swags, and floral festoons. Painted borders enhance the rectilinearity of the panels. Other wall decorations might include cornices and Ionic pilasters, and wainscoting, both real and trompe l'oeil.

To maximize sunlight, windows are quite tall and dressed in delicate white swags. The color palette is airy and delicate, playing off shades of pearl gray, soft blue, and muted tones of pink and yellow. At night, the candle glow radiating from crystal chandeliers reinforces the Swedish preference for an almost ethereal quality of light.

Furnishings are distinguished by slim, tapered, and often channeled legs. Additional decorations include such classical motifs as the egg-and-dart and stylized acanthus leaves that are carved into the wood. Every room would have at least one Gustavian chair, a classic 18th-century chair that has a wooden medallion back with carved flowers at the crown, an upholstered seat (now almost exclusively rendered in checked cotton or linen), and turned legs with stylized carved flowers where the legs meet the seat.

CLOCKWISE FROM FAR LEFT: Mirrored sconces, a crystal chandelier, classically carved table and chairs, and soft colors bring a Gustavian tone to this Stockholm apartment. Painted borders decorate canvas panels affixed to the walls. The golden trompe l'oeil panels were painstakingly restored by Stockholm's Björkstads group after a fire. The trompe l'oeil medallion over the doorway is quintessentially Gustavian.

THE
BEDROOM

THERE ARE FEW IMAGES AS evocative of warmth, security, and earthly bliss as the featherbed. Climb in on a cold winter night, snuggle deeply into the toasty pocket created by a goose down mattress beneath and fluffy comforter above . . . and all your worries melt away.

The Swedish bedroom is as gentle and comforting as the featherbed it so often contains. Pale, muted colors and simple furnishings leave no doubt that the intention here is to create an environment where one can slumber in peace. Is it any surprise that the literal translation of *sovrum*, the Swedish word for bedroom, is *sleep room?*

The purity and simplicity of a Swedish bedroom make it a true sanctuary. Furnishings are minimal and colors are inspired by nature.

WALLS AND FLOORS IN SOOTHING SHADES

In the late 1700s, King Gustav III needed to build a series of guest rooms for the courtiers he expected to entertain at the royal castle of Gripsholm, 60 miles from the capital. In an architectural stroke that still serves as a model for sleeping rooms, the king ordered a wing of twenty-eight identical chambers, each outfitted with a bed, a chest of drawers that was pure and simple of line, a mirror, and two chairs. The floors were plain scrubbed pine and the walls were covered with canvas painted with delicate motifs such as floral wreaths and vines, all rendered in soft, hushed shades. The effect was quiet, uncomplicated, and elegant.

Although painted canvas panels may have deferred to gently sponged walls, the Swedish bedroom of today observes the standards set forth by Gustav 200 years ago. If one is to sleep well, one must first relax. Therefore, the envelope of a room—its ceiling, walls, and floor—should set a soothing tone.

The bedroom's wooden floor, as in the rest of the house, is generally left uncovered, save perhaps for the occasional striped runner. The floorboards are either left in their natural state, or they are whitewashed or painted in a simple

Simplicity can be ever so peaceful. Scrubbed pine floors and powdery soft color-washed walls provide Julia and Isabelle with the perfect retreat.

diamond or checkerboard pattern. The painted patterns particularly suit American homes and are easy to re-create with only the most basic of craft or painting skills.

No matter what the size of the room, the diamonds or checks painted upon the floorboards should be relatively large. If the pattern is scaled too small, it can produce an overly busy look that intrudes upon the sense of calm. Fitting colors to consider: a subdued range of grays and blues, celadons and gray-greens.

An uncomplicated way to evoke the soft feeling so typical of Swedish bedroom walls is to use a color wash that blends two or more diffused colors in a subtle tone-on-tone effect (see page 81). Stay within a narrow range of soft, misty colors drawn from nature: pale sky blue, straw yellow, granite gray, and so on. As an alternative, wash on a single hue; the wall will appear less textured but the process requires less of an investment of your time and creates a pleasing atmosphere.

If you would like to replicate the quiet sophistication of an 18th-century wall, consider a wallpaper that reproduces a classic historical pattern on a white ground (see Sources). For a more ambitious evocation of the elegant Gustavian era, affix canvas to the wall and create your own trompe l'oeil panels with tempera paint (follow our recipe and how-tos for working with tempera, page 176). Canvasing a wall is a job best delegated to a professional; many top-notch painters actually recommend this procedure, especially when the wall in question is a plaster one.

For guidance and inspiration, follow the example of many Swedes and study illustrated books that depict period interiors (see Sources). This is a time-honored aid: to formulate their design ideas, many 18th-century creators of stunning Gustavian rooms first scrutinized engraved plates and drawings of classic Greek and Roman decoration.

White walls remain a perfectly acceptable choice for the bedroom, particularly if you prefer a contemporary look and mood. Another option is narrow stripes. You can paint these directly on the wall or purchase a striped wallpaper. Favorite color combinations are soft blue and white, gray and white, and gray and cream. Or for a more artful look, try pale yellow and gray.

To preserve a peaceful atmosphere, walls and floors should remain free of clutter. In Sweden, one finds little artwork hung in a bedroom. Instead, a wall will be adorned with a mirror over a dresser, a wall lamp for reading next to the bed, and then, perhaps, a single piece of art. Likewise, the floor is unencumbered. Furnishings generally comprise a bed, a chair, a nightstand, and a simple dresser. Even if this inventory seems limited, rooms function well and are actually less sparse than they may sound, because a large storage unit is often built into one wall.

To emulate the color-washed bedroom walls shown on these pages, choose two tones, or values, of a sky blue, light gray, or pale straw yellow. First, roll on a coat of flat latex paint in the paler tone. Allow this undercoat to dry (flat latex will dry with the chalky quality of plaster). Then, using a semigloss latex in the slightly darker value, mix your wash in the following ratio: one-third paint, one-third Floetrol brand or other paint extender, and one-third water. Experiment on heavy white oaktag or poster board, available in art stores, or on a remnant of drywall, to get the color value and degree of runniness you want. Working with a friend, use a 4-inch-wide paintbrush or a large sea sponge and quickly spread the color wash over the base coat, moving your hand in big swirling motions. Have your friend follow you with a piece of cheesecloth or old terry towel and blot the wash to achieve the degree of mottling that you desire.

Opposite: Gisela Montan painted diamonds on the wide planks of her bedroom floor. Note the scale of the diamonds—each measures about two feet across. Below: Painter Hans Yngve bleached the floors of his Stockholm apartment and used a gentle yellow color wash for the walls.

THE BED

Sweden, like France, has a glorious tradition of beautifully canopied beds. In the finest houses the bedrooms were appointed with handsomely carved flying half-testers, nicely turned or hand-carved four-poster beds, or gracious *lits à la polonaise*, with curved supports culminating in crowns. The Swedish beds, however, differed from the French models in three important ways that reflect a preference for simplicity and purity.

First and foremost, bed hangings in all but the most regal of homes were rendered not in silk, but rather in calico or other simple cottons. If the cottons were hand-blocked, motifs typically were printed on a white ground. If woven, the most popular choices were, of course, stripes and checks. For a simpler look, hangings were eliminated altogether and the bed would be covered only with a tailored canopy.

Secondly, Swedish beds are distinguished by the treatment of the wood frame. This was not only beautifully carved but also often painted a pale gray or "English red"—the Swedish name for a reddish-brown color. Lastly, following the Swedish preference for flexible furnishings, the beds could expand and collapse as space needs dictated. The handsomely carved half-tester "imperial" bed, a style popular in Gustavian times, could be compressed to half its length, thanks to an

This reproduction of an 18th-century bed is available from IKEA, and the hangings are copies of a fabric first designed around 1750.

ingeniously designed frame that retracted along gliding rails. (The mattress would fold in half, or be taken off when the bed was shortened.) Some homes were furnished with crown-shaped canopy beds that could be widened by pulling out the side of the bed, echoing the American trundle bed.

Today a wide range of bed styles evokes a Swedish mood. If you prefer a romantic look, consider the canopied styles popular during the 17th and 18th centuries, such as the crown-shaped or rectangular half-testers that attach to the wall over the head of the bed, or a four-poster canopied bed. Select textiles and bed linens in pale shades; soft sky blues and pale yellows or grays are always good options. For the quintessential Swedish tone, choose a motif of classic checks and stripes. For a rustic, country charm, consider a simple headboard and footboard in natural or whitewashed pine. The wood may be carved with the stylized flower or pinecone finials popular in the 18th century; if the carvings are simple, the bed will look correct in its relaxed surroundings.

Beds with white enameled metal frames are favored by many Swedes. Not only do they fit right in with a light mood, but their svelte silhouettes and slatted head- and footboards allow them to marry well with other simple furnishings in the bedroom. Another benefit of metal beds is that they are quite durable. For those whose taste leans toward a spare and contemporary mood, the basic Swedish bed is a fine choice: a simple frame, a mattress with a sheet, a down comforter covered in

a cotton duvet, and two pillows. It's comfortable, practical, and most forgiving in the daily routine of making the bed. Just shake out the comforter, punch the pillows, and the bed is set!

Canopy kits for crownlike half-testers can be found at many home centers or decorating superstores. Or you can make your own. One easy version of the crown tester shown on page 85 can be made from a semicircle of ½-inch-thick plywood. A lumberyard can cut one to the radius you desire. As you would recover a chair seat, use a staple gun to attach cotton batting to the plywood, then upholster it and drape with a typical Swedish cotton fabric. A band of ribbon or fabric trim could replace the wood molding in the photo. Consult your local hardware or home improvement store for the best type of brackets to attach the crown to your wall; if your fabric is heavy, you may need to screw the brackets into molly bolts.

A third option is to work with plaster cherubs, available through many decorating stores and catalogs. One type to consider measures about a foot high, is fashioned with a rounded tunnel through which fabric can be passed, and mounts flat on a wall. Simply center the figure over the head of your bed, attach it to the wall, and pass a length of lightweight cotton through the tunnel, allowing it to drape on either side of the bed. Finally, if your budget permits, a variety of period testers are available in antique stores that can be refitted with reproduction fabrics and installed over your bed (see Sources).

ABOVE: Lars and Ursula Sjöberg designed an exact copy of a Gustavian-era bed. They also designed the printed cotton hangings after an 18th-century fabric. LEFT AND OPPOSITE, TOP: In her New York showroom, Estelle deJounge sells reproductions of classic Swedish beds and canopies. The cotton fabrics are all manufactured in Sweden. OPPOSITE, BOTTOM: Red stripes are a perfect fabric choice for a canopy bed in the *lit à la polonaise* style.

HOW TO **SLEEP**

The secret of a good night's sleep? In Sweden, and most everywhere in Scandinavia, it is a particular configuration of mattresses that evolved from the old featherbeds. Today's version retains the soul-soothing, cuddly comfort of its ancestors but incorporates healthful support for the spine and the neck offered by 20th-century technology. The base of the Swedish bed, which is available in the United States through several manufacturers (see Sources), resembles the box spring we find in most American homes. It sits on a bed frame of wood or metal, measures about 12 inches in depth, and provides a very firm support. This base is then topped by a slim mattress, measuring only about 3 inches in depth and filled with a mixture of goose down, wool, and synthetic fiber padding. It is usually anchored to the bottom mattress by a line of stitching set in from the edge (allowing enough room to tuck in the sheets), or it is kept in place by elasticized bands that slip over each corner of the bottom mattress.

The ultimate in sleeping luxury is then to add a third layer—an old-fashioned featherbed. Resembling a cloudlike mattress-sized pillow, the

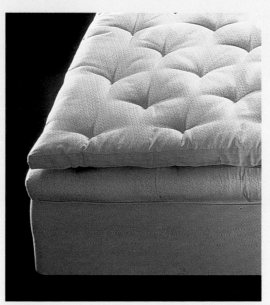

The Duxiana company is renowned for its bed systems—a slim top mattress is anchored by stitching it to a deep, firm foundation. The Swedes claim this is the most healthful and restful way to sleep.

featherbed is made from a mixture of goose feathers and goose down encased in a cotton cover, and sometimes stitched into channel baffles. The greater the ratio of feathers to down, the firmer the bed will be. Featherbeds are widely available in the United States through various mail-order firms, such as The Company Store and Chambers (see Sources). Devotees swear by them, claiming there is no finer way to support each joint, or to provide a toasty cushion of air beneath the body.

How to dress a Swedish bed? Like people in most European countries, the Swedes rarely use fitted sheets. The bed is made with two flat sheets, and because there is no heavy mattress to lift, the job is quick and easy. Finally, a fluffy goose down comforter is placed on top and accompanied by two square pillows. The ensemble all but guarantees the perfect night's sleep. In many homes the duvet cover doubles as a top sheet. Made from a high-quality cotton, the duvet cover has an additional "tail" of fabric at the bottom that tucks neatly under the mattress at the foot of the bed. Come laundry day, the comforter slides out and the sheet can go right into the washing machine.

THE LOWDOWN ON
GOOSE DOWN

All down comforters and featherbeds are not created equally; variances involve issues of quality as well as preference. Down is extolled as a superior insulation material, but why—and what, exactly, is down?

Ironic as it may seem, air is nature's supreme insulator; it is the air pockets in wood or fiberglass insulation, for example, that make a house feel warm. Down grows in soft, fuzzy clusters under the feathers that insulate the bellies of geese and ducks from the cold. Because down resists crushing, it creates thousands of little air pockets. Those air pockets, together with the soft fuzz, provide superior warmth. The added bonus: down weighs almost nothing.

Down clusters vary in terms of size and resiliency, and are graded according to their "fill power." The producer places down in a one-ounce cylinder that is then topped by a specially calibrated weight. The more the down resists the weight, the greater its fill power is said to be. The higher the fill power, the less down you need to achieve your desired level of warmth and the lighter the comforter can be. The best-quality com-

forters will have fill powers ranging from 600 to 750 cubic inches per ounce.

The next factor to consider is the choice of fabric used to cover the down. Tightly woven cotton is said to be "downproof"—meaning the down cannot poke through the weave. Although

cotton sheets (and blends) may be woven with as few as 120 threads per inch, cotton used to contain down should be woven with a minimum of a 200–230 thread count. (Thread count is the industry term defining the numbers of threads per square inch.) Comforters of best quality will start at 230 and run up to about 330. Some of the most densely woven cottons are known as Egyptian cottons.

How a comforter is filled and sewn also determines quality. Two types of construction are preferred: sewn-through or baffle. Both create pockets or channels in the comforter to prevent the down from shifting excessively and creating an area with no insulation, known in the trade as a cold spot. Sewn-

YOUR DREAM OF A ROMANTIC CANOPY NEED NOT INVOLVE THE PURCHASE OF A NEW BED. MANY OPTIONS EXIST, SOME REQUIRING VERY LITTLE INVESTMENT. CONSIDER THE SIMPLE WOODEN DOWEL WITH STAR SHOWN IN THE PHOTOGRAPH, OPPOSITE. THESE ARE AVAILABLE BY MAIL (SEE PAGE 178) OR CAN BE FASHIONED IN A HOME WORKSHOP.

through construction simply means that the comforter is sewn like a quilt, from the top ticking to the bottom ticking. One criticism of sewn-through construction is that it creates places where the top and bottom layers actually touch, thus causing potential cold spots. Baffle construction adds extra walls of fabric that not only prevent the down from shifting but also prevent the two tickings from touching.

Comforters are sold according to the amount of warmth desired. Down naturally adjusts to a sleeper's temperature, but too much down can prove too hot. Generally graded in four or five levels, a down comforter with just a minimal amount of filling will be comfortable on a summer evening with a cool breeze; filled to its maximum, a down comforter will keep a sleeper toasty even on the coldest winter nights.

Caring for your comforter properly will extend its life to three decades or more. Always cover your comforter, even if its own ticking looks and feels just fine. A comforter cover, also called a duvet (the French word for down), protects the ticking from dust, dirt, and perspiration and is easy to wash. Fluff up the comforter regularly and air it out completely at least once a year. Every five to seven years the comforter can be washed by machine, using cool water and a very mild detergent that will not strip the down of its natural lanolins. If you clean the cover regularly, however, the comforter may not need washing. Also, if you think your washing machine may be too

small to accommodate such a large piece, have it professionally dry-cleaned.

Connie Carlson of The Company Store, a manufacturer of down products in La Crosse, Wisconsin, cautions against using any softeners, as they tend to make the filling migrate. Dry the comforter by machine, using a moderate setting. Check on its progress constantly; Carlson advises not to overexpose the comforter. Leave it in the dryer just long enough to refluff the down and remove the dampness. Then let it air-dry.

A light, fluffy down comforter encased in a softly colored cotton cover is the bed cover of choice in Sweden. Weighing only ounces, these comforters will keep a sleeper warm in the heart of the Swedish winter.

A WORD ABOUT
NIGHTSTANDS

The nightstand is one piece of furniture that tends to be particularly delicate in the Swedish home. Judging from carefully preserved 18th-century interiors, nightstands appear to have evolved from two sources. One was the English candlestand, a small round-topped table with a pedestal base that was placed next to the bed to hold a carafe of water, a glass, and a candlestick. The second was a narrow wooden chest standing on slim, tapered legs and set next to the bed to conceal a chamber pot. The top surface served to hold the glass, carafe, and candlestick.

Modern living has obviated the need for storing a chamber pot, and electric lights have replaced the flickering candle, but the aesthetic standards of 18th-century nightstands have endured. The prettiest choices today are either very slim tables, with long tapered legs (and perhaps one shallow drawer), small round pedestal tables, or reproductions of 18th-century chamber pot cabinets such as those available through IKEA. For an appropriately soothing look, the nightstand should be painted in a pale gray, soft blue, or white; a natural blond wood such as beech, ash, or pine is also an excellent choice. Try to limit accessories, perhaps just a lamp, a book, and a water glass.

The style of nightstand you choose plays an important role in defining the look of your bedroom. Lean toward slim, delicate lines and soft colorations.

SOFT **PALETTES**

The pearlescent painted finishes of Swedish antique furnishings grow more resplendent with each passing year. Even objects preserved from the 17th and 18th centuries still boast magnificent patinas that have worn gently but never chipped. What is the secret to these exquisite painted finishes? "The most beautiful of them were achieved with egg tempera paint," says Ralph Edenheim, author of the book *Skansen* and a scholar-in-residence at Stockholm's famous open-air museum of the same name, to which many historic Swedish homes have been relocated. Egg tempera paint has been used for more than three centuries in Sweden. "It is simply a mixture of egg, linseed oil, and powdered pigment," Edenheim explains. "It is all natural, long-lasting, nontoxic, and sublimely beautiful."

To learn more about time-honored Swedish painting techniques, I met with Edenheim and his wife, Katarina, also a scholar of Swedish decorative arts, at the 18th-century house they occupy on the grounds of Skansen. Though their home is brimming with the books and historical artifacts typical of an intellectual couple, Katarina and Ralph do not confine their activity to

intellectual pursuits. They are "hands-on" historians, having personally mixed the paint that decorates every surface of their impeccably restored home.

"I think people are overwhelmed at the notion of mixing their own paint," says Ralph, "but actually, nothing could be easier." To prove his point, he pulled a small table out from the wall, protected the surface with paper, and assembled the tools of his trade: a wire whisk, a few fresh eggs, a bottle of boiled linseed oil, water, and some jars of powdered pigment. (Linseed oil and pigment are available

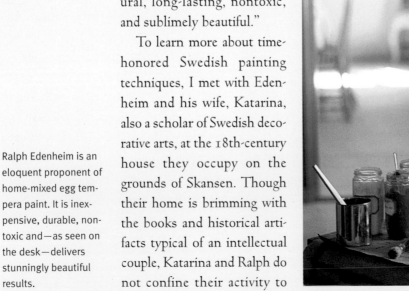

Ralph Edenheim is an eloquent proponent of home-mixed egg tempera paint. It is inexpensive, durable, nontoxic and—as seen on the desk—delivers stunningly beautiful results.

The ingredients of egg tempera are simple: fresh eggs, boiled linseed oil, powdered pigment, and water. ABOVE: Ralph Edenheim and his wife, Katarina, painted this reproduction 18th-century chair, emulating the "English red" popular during the Gustavian era. OPPOSITE: On the interior walls of their 18th-century home, Ralph and Katarina have exclusively used distemper paint that they mixed themselves.

at art supplies stores.) He cracked one egg into a small bowl, added 2 ounces of the oil and 2 ounces of water, and whisked them together. He then measured 2 tablespoons of red cinnabar, a powdered pigment, and added it to the egg-oil/water base. Picking up a rounded bristle brush, Edenheim applied the just-mixed paint to a scrap of wood. The paint glimmered with a rich yet delicate luminescence.

The Swedes have long relied on this simple method of creating egg tempera to paint and decorate furniture. "It requires a little patience," notes Edenheim, "because it must be put on in very thin layers and it takes a while to dry." But the rewards are worth the effort. Not only is egg tempera unmatched for its pearly smooth surface, which can be buffed to a fine sheen, but it literally lasts a lifetime.

The recipe for egg tempera painting varies slightly from region to region. Some painters add a few drops of mineral spirits (see "Paint Recipes," page 176). Take appropriate caution, however, if you decide to include a chemical-based paint thinner in your blend. Keep small children away from your work area, and make sure to provide adequate ventilation to counteract the fumes.

Generally, egg tempera paints are used only for furniture. For larger surfaces such as interior walls, a less expensive paint called "distemper" is used. Pigment, chalk (or whiting, as it is sometimes called), water, and rabbit-skin glue are mixed to yield distemper. The result is an appealingly soft and powdery look; however, the pigment has a tendency to rub off a bit. (See page 176.)

For some painting projects, Ralph and Katarina Edenheim like to modify the final finish with a glaze. Glazes can be used both to soften or to intensify a base color. In these instances, they use the egg, water, and boiled linseed oil just as in the egg tempera mix. But only a hint of pigment is added, perhaps just a teaspoon of cinnabar powder, depending upon the look they want. When applied, it gives the surface a beautiful, translucent sheen (see page 176).

The study of exterior painting techniques has led Edenheim to some of his more intriguing theories. One story he relates concerns the so-called Falun red, a color found on the exteriors of many Swedish homes. A dark red paint based on the rich stores of iron oxide found in the central Sweden town of the same name, Falun red is made from heating rye meal, iron sulfate, and iron oxide powder. The Swedes believe it has a special, almost magical ability to protect wood from anything that might weaken it. But pointing to the fact that most Swedish wooden houses went unpainted until the 19th century, Edenheim argues that the real impetus for the color's popularity was fashion. As evidence, he points to the

House of Nobilities, a brick mansion designed by a Dutch architect and erected in Stockholm during the 1670s to resemble the much coveted stately homes in Holland. Although building with brick was out of reach for all but the wealthiest Swedes, painting one's house the color of brick was not. Once the upper classes started to embrace Falun red, it was only a matter of time before the practice became widespread.

Another popular exterior color (although a distant second to Falun red) is yellow. During his travels to Italy, Nicodemus Tessin the Younger (architect to Gustav III and creator of the Royal Palace in Stockholm) was inspired by the yellow plaster sheathing of the villas he saw in Rome. He first introduced the color in Sweden by constructing stone houses and painting them yellow. Other Swedes took to imitating the look simply by painting their wooden structures in the appropriate soft yellow and then adding trompe l'oeil "columns" and "pilasters" for authenticity.

As proponents of the value of traditional Swedish painting, Ralph and Katarina spend several weeks each year traveling throughout the country teaching new generations of artists and craftspeople how to master the time-proven techniques. Their message is a potent one: beautiful, practical, and ecologically safe paints are within everyone's grasp. Nature has provided the key elements. All we need supply is imagination—and elbow grease.

RIGHT: The enfilade
design of the
Edenheims' 18th-
century home creates
a pleasing spectrum of
color. OPPOSITE:
Katarina's grandmother
embroidered the cloth
that graces the tea
table.

NATURAL
HUES

To understand the colors of
Sweden, one need only cast an
eye across the serene and subtle hues imparted by the landscape. The quintessential pale
grays, powder-soft blues, deep
reds, and buttery yellows seem
to leap directly from field and
meadow, rock and ocean, into
the tranquil, inviting interiors.

CARL LARSSON

At all too rare intervals, the world is blessed with an artist who can paint the contours of happiness: the delight of a child, the pride of a parent, the love of a husband for his wife. Carl Larsson, a complex man forged by poverty and pain and revisited throughout his life by dark moments, transcended the gravity of suffering to fully appreciate the beauty around him. As Sweden's most famous and most beloved artist, Larsson's life's work, and notably his watercolor depictions of family life, have come to symbolize the Swedish ideals of hearth and home, and stand as a beacon of Swedish national pride.

Carl Larsson was born in Stockholm in May 1853 and faced a difficult childhood. His father was abusive and never able to support the family. They moved continually from one vermin-infested dwelling to the next, while his mother took in laundry to sustain a meager supply of food. Even in those early and difficult days, however, Carl showed artistic promise, drawing sketches in the margins of old bookkeeping books. As an adolescent, he entered the Swedish Academy of Fine Arts, and at the age of twenty-three, he went to France, where he met Karin Bergöö, another young Swedish artist. They married in Sweden in 1883 and then returned to France for two years to live in an artist colony in the village of Grez, just south of Paris. By this time, Larsson had started to earn recognition for his art. He received the Royal Medal from the Academy of Art in Stockholm and, equally important, his paintings began to sell.

In 1888, Karin's father gave the young couple a small cottage called "Lilla Hyttnäs," in the town of Sundborn in the province of Dalarna. Thrilled, Carl and Karin spent their spare time and meager savings rehabilitating the dwelling. Three years later, they moved to the cottage on a full-time basis. There they found the freedom to express their own tastes and to create a bright and cozy environment for their family of seven children.

Karin proved to be a brilliant artisan. She designed and wove textiles of stunning originality. Bed hangings, tapestries, table runners, and more, woven on her loom, still look contemporary almost a century after their creation. Carl Larsson approached the house as a three-dimensional canvas, painting and embellishing every nook and cranny. Combining Swedish peasant traditions with the sophisticated techniques he had studied in France, he created a marvelous blend of winsome charm and classical refinement.

The decoration of Lilla Hyttnäs had a

Carl Larsson painting at his home, Lilla Hyttnäs. His wife, Karin, was one of Larsson's favorite models.

Both Carl and Karin
Larsson were talented
artists, using their
skills for painting,
weaving, and design-
ing to create intimacy
and charm in every
room of their family
home in Sundborn.

profound effect on homes at every level of Swedish society. As with other artists working at the turn of the century in what came to be known as the Arts and Crafts movement—or, in Sweden, the National Romantic movement—the Larssons offered encouragement in resisting the mechanization of life that had been catalyzed by the Industrial Revolution. They advocated a simple, home-focused life where the goals were to use one's hands, imagination, and natural materials to create a personalized environment. The Larssons became a sort of ideal couple, upon whom many Swedes modeled their own aspirations and values.

Although Larsson earned his income during these first years at Lilla Hyttnäs by illustrating books and accepting commissions for murals and other civic projects, he satisfied his spontaneous artistic impulses by sketching the little scenes of daily life that were played out by the members of his own family. "I simply could not stay away from putting down on paper all these funny and cute little scenes that were constantly before my eyes," he wrote in his autobiography. A first collection of watercolors, *De Mina* (*My Loved Ones*) appeared in 1895, but it was the publication of *Ett Hem* (*A Home*) in 1899 that firmly established Larsson's reputation.

During a few rainy summer weeks, Karin suggested to her husband that he create a visual record of each room in the house. Sketching empty rooms felt too sterile to him, so Larsson added a bit of life by putting one child or another into each tableau. Their friend the Swedish artist Anders Zorn took the first dozen canvases and brought them to America to be part of a traveling exhibit of Swedish art. The pictures were an instant and enormous success, and the eminent Swedish publisher Albert Bonnier urged Larsson to create a text that could accompany the images. "I blushed more than once," Larsson would recall, "ashamed of so unabashedly . . . bragging about my home, my wife, and my children . . . [but] perhaps this is why it became the most . . . lasting part of my life's work. For these pictures are a . . . very genuine expression of . . . all my limitless love for my wife and children."

In the seventh decade of his richly textured life, Larsson recorded his memoirs. He had known abject poverty, had contemplated suicide, and had done many things of which he was not proud. But he maintained an unbending faith in God and wrote movingly, "When I was close to fading, you, God and Father of us all, kindled my fire and filled me with your limitless love. . . . I have always wanted to do what is right, and I have sought the nobility of spirit. . . . I will never pray for forgiveness for my sins. I want to do my penance honestly. . . . But I am not afraid. I have loved." Two days later, Larsson died.

THE
DINING
ROOM

OVER A FEAST OF FRESHLY caught and grilled sea bass, the voices of designer Anika Reuterswärd, her husband, and grown children join to offer a spirited rendition of "Helan Går," one of the most beloved of Swedish toasting songs. In their home, as in homes all over Sweden, the dining room is often filled with song.

Swedes adore entertaining friends around the table and always imbue the experience with good humor. Witty toasts and engaging

The Swedish dining room is a charming and elegant model of restraint.

stories mingle with hearty laughter—
and, of course, delicious food and drink—
to make the dining room one of the
favorite gathering places in the home.

A MOST
CONGENIAL SPOT

Like other rooms in the Swedish home,
the dining room is a delightfully graceful
and airy place. Its furnishings may range
in style from elegant blond Swedish Biedermeier to rustic whitewashed pine,
but the ensemble is always inviting.
This appealing spirit can easily be re-
created in any home by selecting furnishings and a color scheme that reflect
the soft hues and lithe silhouettes preferred by the Swedes.

First and foremost, choose a table and
chairs crafted of a light or painted wood.
The dining table should present a graceful profile, with tapered or turned legs; the
chairs should be constructed with slat
backs. In rare instances one may find
upholstered straight-back dining chairs in
a Swedish home, but they will have slender contours and will often be upholstered with a vertically striped fabric that
visually mutes their presence.

As in other rooms, the walls, floors,
and ceilings should be rendered in pale,
natural hues. Take care not to overburden

Charlotte Bonnier's dining room makes visitors
swoon with nostalgia for the simpler life of days
past. The Larsson-style lamp, soft diamond-
painted floor, and crisp white linens work brilliantly in her seaside home.

Gaga Bonnier is very
fond of the Swedish
Biedermeier style. She
had the leafy trellis
design painted to com-
plement the soft blond
wood furnishings of
her dining room.

ABOVE: A pristine atmosphere is created by using white for all painted surfaces and furnishings. When accented by blue dinnerware the effect is crisp, modern, and very pleasing.

RIGHT: Open-back chairs confer a light and graceful mood in the dining room of antique dealer Babbi Wallenberg.

the walls. Ceilings are best painted white, or alternatively a very light color. In most Swedish homes the wood floors are left uncovered, which allows the fine silvery gray or whitewashed planks to enhance the airy mood of the room. If you have wooden floors, consider bleaching them, or painting them so that they will be in harmony with the walls.

Other furnishings in the room, if there are any, should be limited and practical. The table and chairs may be complemented with a hutch or a sideboard in a compatible light-toned or painted wood. A favorite decoration for sideboards in Sweden is vertically carved channels on the cabinet doors. Remember, to help lighten its visual presence, the sideboard will always sit on legs.

SMART **TABLES**

Because tables can be voracious consumers of space, the Swedes have long insisted on "smart tables"—tables that are there when you need them, and out of the way when you don't. More precisely, this means that a table has to collapse, allowing it to be stored at the periphery of the room when not in use. Furthermore, the table must be designed and constructed so that it offers the option of various configurations, depending upon the surface area needed. Ideally, it is also modular, so that several units can be joined to form one expansive surface.

Even in the stately homes of the 18th century, where space was not restricted, the preference for this type of flexible table held firm. The motivation was aesthetic: Swedes of every economic bracket have always believed that a graceful and pleas-

ing feeling is created when the center of a room is kept open and free of furniture. The smart table gave them a means to their desired end.

Any home, and particularly smaller apartments, will gain space and flexibility by favoring these smart tables. The simplest type is a round dining table that divides into two freestanding units. Each half-round stands on three legs, thus being perfectly stable when returned to a parking place against the wall. A round table with a tilting top is another popular choice; when abutting the wall, it takes up virtually no floor space.

The most popular table of all is, and always has been, the double gateleg. Two sets of legs pivot 45 degrees from the midline table base to support two drop leaves. When the leaves drop, they hide the base, thus transforming the table into a console. The narrow center board capping the base serves as the top for the console when the table is pushed against the wall. In addition to its use as a console, the gateleg table can be used halfway open, with one dropped leaf placed flat against the wall, or it can be positioned between two half-rounds to make a very large extended oval table. Companies such as IKEA and Pottery Barn sell gateleg tables that have an enclosed chamber around the central legs with storage space for four folding chairs—a smart table indeed.

OPPOSITE: Anika Reuterswärd designed this table to be as beautiful as it is practical. Extra leaves slide out from under the table to provide a sturdy work surface. BELOW: Space savers par excellence: a round table divides into two freestanding units. The double gateleg table can be used with one or both leaves up yet stores against a wall, occupying just a foot of space.

SETTING
THE TABLE

Like an accomplished actor who can transform him- or herself into a remarkable range of characters, the Swedish table boasts an extraordinary repertoire. With beguiling simplicity, an uncovered wooden table can be laid with creamy dinnerware accompanied by cotton napkins in a blue-and-white check. But, as any Nobel laureate will attest, Sweden has an exquisitely refined side to her traditions of hospitality as well. Indeed, Sweden is one of the last countries in Europe to maintain the tradition of the *Frack*—white tie and tails—not only for the annual Nobel Prize awards banquet but for all formal academic and royal occasions.

The key to creating a Swedish feeling at your table is to understand the importance of paring away the superficial to arrive at the essence of an object's beauty. Less *is* more. A beautiful tablecloth can be very plain—simply and superbly woven from finely spun unbleached linen. It need not rely upon a special print, pattern, or coloration to be appealing, or be adorned with any fancy trimming. Indeed, embellishment of any sort could not render beautiful a cloth that was not already expertly woven.

If the occasion, or your preference, calls for a casual style, look to nature, and especially the beauty of wood, for inspiration. In Sweden, it is perfectly appropriate to serve any meal on a bare wooden table. Place mats are neither necessary nor expected. Charming settings can be created with glazed earthenware, a pretty glass tumbler or a trumpet-shaped schnapps glass, simple flatware, a checked linen napkin, and perhaps some ferns and Queen Anne's lace gathered from the field or roadside and placed in a crackle-glazed vase. Nothing should shout for attention, or jockey for position in a crowded setting. Only two things matter: choose uncomplicated forms, and

RIGHT: Trumpet-shaped glasses are used for both wine and schnapps in Sweden. These are copies of 18th-century glasses now being produced by IKEA. ABOVE: Admired for their intrinsic beauty, wooden tables are often left uncovered.

stick to the soft colors found in nature.

At the formal end of the spectrum, a close look at the Nobel Prize awards table setting serves as a delightful tutorial in the Swedish art of table dressing, revealing in the most exquisite manner the aesthetic preferences of Swedish culture.

The current Nobel setting was created by art historian Åke Livstedt and designer Magnus Silverhjelm for the ninetieth anniversary of the award in 1991. Livstedt is an expert on traditional Swedish protocol and ceremony as well as on vintage porcelain, crystal, and other adornments for the table. Not only was the table to provide an elegant backdrop for the prestigious awards, but it was also to remain loyal to the time-honored *konsthantverken*—the artisanal handicrafts deeply rooted in Sweden's past.

The foundation of the setting comes from Klässbols Linneväveri, weavers of traditional damasks based in Vårmland, in the center of Sweden. Coarse silvery gray linen thread was woven into a large-scale, tone-on-tone, irregular basketweave pattern for the tablecloth. The dinner napkins were crafted from half-bleached linen thread in a slightly paler tone. Each napkin was adorned with a relief medallion showcasing the Nobel medal. Together, the napkins and tablecloth create an elegant yet natural tone for the table.

Sweden's oldest manufacturer of porcelains, Rörstrand, founded in 1726, was commissioned to fabricate the dinner service. The dinner plates are a pure bone color, white rimmed with gold. Smaller plates used for the first course add a hint

LEFT: Weavers at Klässbols prove how beautiful a simple silver-gray linen thread can look when handled with expert care. OPPOSITE, TOP: Three of the grandest names in Swedish tableware, Rörstrand, Orrefors, and GENSE combined forces to create each place setting. OPPOSITE, BOTTOM: The setting for the annual Nobel Prize banquet provides a glorious example of the refinement of Swedish table arts.

of soft spring green as a band just inside the gold rim. The lidded soup bowls are again bone white, and each is topped with a crown, signifying abundance, fertility, and intellect. Companion pieces include shell-shaped salt and pepper dishes—given the delightful name "the Birth of Venus"—and a Rococo-inspired wing-shaped salad plate. It is interesting to note that even in this rarefied setting, the gifts of nature—the green of spring, the wing of a bird, the shell from the sea—make their impression.

Artisan Gustaf Eriksson, of NySilver-fabriken (or GENSE, as the company is known), created the flatware. The cutlery, including a gold-plated fish-shaped knife with a ceramic green eye, was inspired by the table silver belonging to Carl Johan XIV, who reigned as king in the 18th century. Eriksson's version is timeless; its clean lines belong to no century in particular, only to good taste.

Sweden's famed Orrefors Glassworks was responsible for the crystal. All the pieces at the table were handblown at the Orrefors workshops or, under supervi-

sion, in other small glassworks in Små-land, the southernmost province of Sweden, which is renowned for the beauty and quality of its handblown glass. The Orrefors crystal, like the Rörstrand porcelain, encapsulates myriad inspirations from nature. The glass for white wine features a spring green stem that undulates like the waves in the sea. It is nicely complemented by a champagne flute supported by a gold orbed stem; the glass for red wine also rises from a gold stem. A simple, unpretentious water tumbler sits next to these delicate hand-blown creations.

What is so striking about this stunning setting, and so indicative of Swedish values, is the rigorous discipline of each individual design. Because each element of the setting is free from superfluous ornament or garish decoration, it could work for virtually any occasion, from a cozy dinner with friends to a gala wedding reception. The Swedes have shown us that respect for the essential qualities of any object, combined with sensitivity to the gifts of nature, creates beautiful tables.

GIFTS FROM THE GARDEN

That softly rounded stone sitting in the corner of your flowerbed may appear unassuming, but it holds the potential to be an enchanting new place card at your next luncheon party. With a few deft strokes of a paintbrush, you can transform that stone from something prosaic into an ornament to enhance your table setting.

Follow the example of designer Anika Reuterswärd, who set the stunning table on these pages with things she and her family collected on the property outside their country home. A lovely natural linen cloth anchors the tablescape. A centerpiece was created using a wooden decoy normally found in the living room. An abandoned bird's nest cradling an egg from the kitchen, a few large pebbles washed smooth by the ocean tide, and little pillows of spongy green moss nestle up against the decoy. Anika painted similar rocks with the names of her guests and placed them by the plates. A few feathery green ferns were laid here and there to complete the soft, natural look.

This "ballet of nature" knows no boundaries. Almost anything that strikes you as beautiful can be plucked or harvested from your yard and woven into an inviting table setting.

MAKING THINGS
CRYSTAL
CLEAR

The Swedes didn't invent the art of glassmaking, they just put their own special stamp on it. Swedish glass looks as if it sprang directly from the Scandinavian landscape. The graceful shapes of nature—the cool tactility of a spring-fed lake, the ripples on the water's surface when the breeze blows, the smooth and brilliant opacity of winter ice—are the inspirations that nourish the creations of Sweden's master glass designers.

The heart of Swedish glassmaking is found in the country's southernmost province of Småland, a 4½-hour trip by car south of Stockholm.

Here, set among many picturesque villages, is the tiny hamlet of Orrefors, home to the world-renowned glassworks of the same name. Founded as an ironworks in 1726, Orrefors converted to glass production in 1898 and recently merged with Sweden's oldest glassworks, Kosta Boda.

Småland is God's country; lush spruce forests are punctuated by open meadows dotted with wildflowers and lined with ancient stone walls. Neat wooden houses painted "Falun red" and set off by white picket fences line the village streets. In such idyllic surroundings, it is not hard to imagine why the best of Sweden's glass designers

Imperial by Erika Lagerbielke.

are happy and productive working here.

As entrancing as this bucolic setting is, the real action in Orrefors takes place on the workshop floor, where the thundering clay furnaces or "pots" convert sand, red lead, and sodium carbonate into a molten yellow mass called "melt" that is then suffused with air and cajoled into breathtaking crystal objects.

The transformation from melt to object is rapid—often a couple of minutes or less—so that a precise choreography is needed to integrate all phases of the production into one seamless process. At Orrefors, a team consists of three to seven glassblowers. Many of these skilled artisans represent the third or fourth generation of their families to work at the craft.

It was in 1925, at the Paris Exhibition, that Orrefors—and, by extension, Swedish crystal—first came to the world's attention. An engraved glass goblet designed by portrait and landscape painter Simon Gate for Orrefors took the grand prize. Another artist, Edward Hald, who had studied with Matisse and was also employed by Orrefors, received similar acclaim.

Prior to this time, crystal objects were designed by the glassblowers who made them, but neither Gate nor Hald was trained in the craft. Their arrival on the scene heralded a new development in the making of crystal, with an emphasis now placed on teams creating the various pieces.

A particularly important contribution of Gate and Hald was the development

Wish by Gunnar Cyrén.

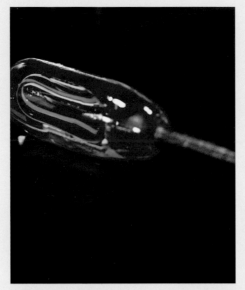

Molten glass is pressed against a horizontal iron plate to give it a preliminary shape. Because the glowing mass must stay in motion, the glassmaker constantly twirls the iron pipe as he shapes the object. A viscous flow of glass is attached to the bowl of a vase and then snipped with scissors. The added glass is then coaxed into the shape of the final base.

in 1916 of the Graal technique, which actually encloses a decorated inner layer of glass in the finished glass object itself. In the 1930s, Orrefors artist Edwin Öhrström developed the Ariel technique, which involves encapsulating a layer of air over a sandblasted design executed on several thin layers of colored glass.

Painters, sculptors, and other artists who came to Orrefors continued to expand the repertoire of glass design, always, of course, relying upon the hands of master glassblowers to realize their designs. Today at Orrefors, a group of eight artists works with the skilled blowers, making designs for art glass as well as glass for everyday use.

TOP LEFT: Martti Rytkönen's playful design features primitively shaped wolves frolicking on a snowy hill. TOP RIGHT: An Orrefors classic—a little girl gazes at the moon. BOTTOM LEFT: With a wink to Eve, Lena Bergström designed this solid apple core. BOTTOM RIGHT: Jan Johansson's petal bowl.

While the advances in dimmer switches, bulbs, and other electric fixtures have been nothing short of astounding, the most romantic and flattering light still comes from a softly dancing flame. For a truly magical setting, select a chandelier and sconces that use only wax candles.

LIGHTING

The evening hours bring a special magic to the Swedish dining room. Soft streams of light flow from the chandelier, sconces, and candlesticks to suffuse the room with warmth. Although each source of light is important in creating this deliciously romantic atmosphere, the shimmering chandelier will always steal the scene.

Crystal chandeliers are not particular to Sweden, but the Swedes seem especially talented at crafting these beautiful creations. Capturing the very essence of the culture's aesthetic, a crystal chandelier—light, airy, and graceful, with twinkling crystals that recall the luminous icicles found in nature—holds pride of place over the dining table in homes both stately and modest.

The evolution of the crystal chandelier dates back to the middle of the 17th century. British art historian Robert Thornton has documented fixtures made from rock crystal mounted on wire armatures, clearly the precursors of the crystal chandeliers that flourished in elegant homes during the latter part of the 17th century and on into the 18th. Though variations on the theme are endless, two particular models stand out as excellent choices for re-creating the dazzling candlelight displays of the 18th century. One type (shown on page 128) became quite

A delicious warmth suffuses the Stockholm dining room of Ralph and Katarina Edenheim. Without a lightbulb in sight (the room has no electricity), a soft light tumbles from candles placed at three different levels.

OPPOSITE: Snowflake-
and star-shaped crys-
tals are among the
most classic forms for
Swedish chandeliers.
INSET: A hand-painted
ceramic tile was
refashioned into a
wall sconce. BELOW: A
forged iron, bell-
shaped chandelier
lends a rustic note to
this room.

fashionable during the Rococo period, and is shaped like an urn. It features crystals in the form of leaves, diamonds, or daisies, anchored by a central faceted, spherical crystal that recalls the early brass chandeliers seen in Dutch interiors. Candles are held by brass mounts. Today's versions often include small electric lights placed inside the body of the chandelier that can be regulated by dimmer switches to augment the candles. For an exquisitely romantic mood, however, try to find a model that uses only candles.

The other type, usually referred to as Gustavian-style (shown on page 131), gives the impression of a flowing fountain. A multitiered crown-shaped top perches on a conical body. Crystal beads are closely strung together so that they tumble in graceful streams terminating in a ring of teardrops. A circular brass frame with brass mounts supports six to eight candles.

There are other choices of chandeliers, of course, that can re-create the pleasing mood of a Swedish dining room, if neither of these models feels appropriate to your home. One, called an "ormolu" chandelier, became popular during the Empire period of the early 19th century. Ormolu refers to gold mounts (in French, *or* means gold, and *moulu* means ground). Often these chandeliers feature a body of darkened bronze shaped as a shallow dish or inverted helmet. They are particularly attractive when paired with Swedish Biedermeier furnishings. Another popular type, one that is unsurpassed for creating a warm, rustic look, is the wrought-iron chandelier crafted in a graceful birdcage-like form.

Working with the chandelier to create the proper dining room lighting are the wall sconce and, most important, the

mirrored sconce. In the middle 1600s mirrored sconces were often used throughout the palaces of Europe to reflect and amplify the candlelight in a room. In Swedish interiors, however, the mirrored sconce dates back only to the Gustavian period, or the late 18th century. Even then they were found only in the finest homes, because the mirrored glass was so difficult to make and the rectangular gold leaf frames with brass candle mounts were so costly. Fortunately, with the advent of modern manufacturing processes, mirrored sconces became widely available, and today the most beloved forms are reproductions of the classic Gustavian models (see Sources). Candlelight flickering off the mirror and dancing on the gilded frame beautifully enriches the dinner atmosphere at the evening meal.

Wall sconces can also be fashioned with beautiful crystals, such as the one pictured on page 133. From simple models that hold one candle to more elaborate versions that hold two or more, a crystal sconce adds a graceful and delicate accent to the room. Sconces need not be elaborate, however, to provide the right blend of light. Simple brass plates or designs made from wrought iron will both contribute to the proper balance of light and add a note of rustic charm.

Finally, completing the balance of

In her home in Westport, Connecticut, Estelle deJounge has re-created the essential light sources of her native Sweden: a crystal chandelier, a pair of silver candlesticks, and simple wall sconces.

TO BRIGHTEN A RAINY AFTERNOON,
PLACE TWO CANDLESTICKS ON THE
LUNCH TABLE AND PUT A CREAMY WHITE
CANDLE IN EACH. AS YOU LIGHT THE
WICKS, WATCH THE GRAYNESS OUTSIDE
THE WINDOW MELT AWAY.

light, no Swedish table setting would be complete without a pair of candlesticks or a candelabrum. Either may be fashioned in silver or crystal, depending upon the preference of the home owner. They often feature crystal bobeches that fit around the candle base to ensure that no wax drips onto the tablecloth.

CANDLES

A single candle with its gently flickering flame is a most evocative image. Depending on the moment and the mood, a lighted candle can instantly convey warmth, welcome, coziness, elegance, or romance. And nowhere are the enchanting qualities of candles more appreciated than Sweden. Virtually every household stocks candles by the dozens and boasts a dazzling variety of candlesticks in which to use them. "The first thing I do on fall and winter mornings," says writer Lena Rydin, "is light the candle on my windowsill. Then I can start my day."

OPPOSITE: What do you get when you mix equal parts respect for the environment and an insatiable appetite for candlelight? A *Stumpastaken*. This clever Swedish invention recycles aluminum cans into a muffin-tin type of platter that has room for sixteen candle nubs. ABOVE AND RIGHT: Candlelight glows just as magically from forms both simple and elegant.

It is hard to imagine, observing the seemingly countless flickerings in modern Swedish homes, that candles did not always appear in such prolific quantities. But until the 20th century, wax candles were quite expensive, so it was rare to see more than a single candlestick in domestic use.

This need to conserve can clearly be seen in all chandeliers built through the 19th century. A *stumpalustre*, a single candle placed in the bottom of the chandelier, and not the four or six candles held by the brass mounts, was the only source of light in the dining room on all but the grandest occasions. Also reflecting the value of candles well into the 20th century was one of the festive activities of Christmas, when neighbors would gather to melt all their collected candle nubs and fashion new candles for the winter holidays.

Today, in addition to the candles that are lit just to bring a bit of beauty to daily life, special types of candles mark various holidays and functions. Pastel-colored candles are used at Eastertime, and for Christmas, candle wax is fashioned in the shape of a candelabrum: five arms rise from a single stem.

Candlesticks can also be holiday specific, such as the one used to hold the four Advent candles, or the crown-shaped holder worn by the young girl chosen to lead the Santa Lucia procession in mid-December.

BELOW: This angelic doll is the traditional candle decoration for the mid-December celebration of Santa Lucia. RIGHT: Clear glass candlesticks enhance the purity of the candlelight.

JOSEF FRANK

Furnishings and fabrics designed by Josef Frank look as fresh and appealing today as when he began his work almost a century ago. Frank is identified with Sweden as a result of his 33-year association with the famous Swedish home furnishings store Svenskt Tenn and its founder, Estrid Ericson. He was born, however, in Austria, in 1885, and did not move to Sweden until 1934, when Hitler's rising power rendered untenable his life in Vienna.

Josef Frank's professional training began at the age of eighteen when he entered Vienna's prestigious Institute of Technology to study architecture. Like the city around him, which was lit by the brilliance of such talents as Gustav Mahler, Oskar Kokoschka, Sigmund Freud, and Walter Gropius, Frank's life reflected a dynamic tension between the classical and the avant-garde.

The collapse of the Hapsburg Empire and the ensuing hardship suffered by his countrymen during the 1920s served not only to forge Frank's liberal political leanings but also to define his early architectural projects, and eventually, his "people friendly" approach to furniture design. Involved with the *Siedlung* movement, which worked to erect housing for low-income families, Frank designed buildings that displayed the clean, cubic, unornamented lines of a sworn Functionalist. His interior furnishings, by contrast, broke sharply with the Functionalist dogma. Josef Frank was a champion of home as a place of comfort, where human needs should come first. He warned that allowing an aesthetic ideal to become a tool for standardizing people's living rooms amounted to "barbarism."

In 1925, Frank and an Austrian colleague, Oskar Wlach, founded their own design firm. Calling it *"Haus & Garten"* (House and Garden), they focused their energy on furniture and textile design, with the credo that furniture was to be used and not just admired. That same year, they entered some of their work in the World Exhibition held in Paris. They received an exceedingly positive response; as one contemporary critic wrote, "One is unlikely at present to find anywhere in Europe a significant production which does more than theirs to realize what is healthiest and most viable in the modern spirit."

Estrid Ericson, an artist who had founded her firm, Svenskt Tenn, eight years earlier, won a medal for her pewter designs at this same exhibition. While certainly aware of her future partner, she did not meet him until 1932, when she contacted Frank to request some of his furniture designs. Two years later, Frank moved to Sweden to join Ericson at Svenskt Tenn and three years after that, they returned to the next Paris World Exhibition—this time with a joint entry. The overwhelmingly positive response to their designs affirmed the wisdom of their artistic partnership.

BELOW: Josef Frank and longtime business partner Estrid Ericson. OPPOSITE: Frank designed the furnishings and fabrics for this room in 1955, demonstrating clearly the timeless nature of his work. Characteristically, white walls form the backdrop for his fabric, La Plata.

Throughout his career, Josef Frank retained the ability to remain open to myriad international influences while never losing sight of his own aesthetic vision. In creating his signature look, which was distinctively light, graceful, and clean of silhouette, he acknowledged forms that inspired him along the way: the slim lines and slat backs of Chippendale chairs, the use of cane and bamboo from the Far East, touches of marble and travertine from Italy.

Frank will long be remembered for his dramatic textile designs rendered in cretonne. An unpolished chintz, cretonne takes color very well, making it the perfect canvas for Frank's vivid and imaginative scenes of Paradise, with flowering trees laden with fruit, teeming with exotic birds and butterflies. (See "Checks and Stripes Forever," page 62.)

Josef Frank died in Stockholm in 1967 at the age of eighty-one. His furniture and textile designs, available internationally, continue to be manufactured and sold by Svenskt Tenn.

OPPOSITE: One of Frank's most famous fabrics, Vegetable Tree, adorns the window. BOTTOM LEFT: Botanical motifs were used to decorate the Florabyrån chest, designed in 1950. BOTTOM RIGHT: A glass vitrine appears to float effortlessly above its slender base.

SELECTING
THE DINING
ROOM **CHAIR**

Finding a chair that will capture the qualities of lightness and grace so typical of Swedish homes brings you once again to that country's penchant for marrying beauty with practicality. The chair that typifies many settings is gracefully proportioned yet sturdy, and consumes little space while providing a comfortable place at the table.

The elements always present are an exposed wooden frame and slat back. Other common features include carved decoration in the form of small flowers, shells, or channels; an upholstered drop-in seat;

OPPOSITE: Dining chairs are often draped with short cotton skirts to protect a newly upholstered seat or give life to a worn one. THIS PAGE: Furniture maker Ulf Gustafsson fashions reproductions of 18th-century chairs in his workshop outside of Stockholm. These designs remain very popular today, reflecting the continued preference for furnishings with light, elegant forms.

and legs often fluted and stabilized by stretchers. While perhaps a majority of Swedish dining chairs are painted in a light hue or fashioned from a blond wood, it is by no means rare to see a darker color such as the deep reddish-brown known as English Red.

KEEPING **WARM**

Some inventions, like the dishwasher, make home life a little more convenient. Others literally change the way we live. In 1767 two Swedes, Carl Johan Cronstedt and Fabian Wrede, designed a new type of ceramic tile stove that was so much more efficient at heating a room than an open fireplace that Swedes could now comfortably venture beyond the big kitchen hearth that had until then supplied the only sufficient heat during the long winter. Consequently, the decoration of dining rooms, living rooms, and even bedrooms now flourished as spaces that could be fully used twelve months a year.

The genius of Cronstedt and Wrede's stove was its intricate system of flues and ducts that threaded their way through heat-retaining bricks. The stove was able to capture and use 85 percent of the heat generated in the fire, rendering it eight times more efficient than an open fireplace. To stoke the stove with firewood, only a small opening was required; more ceramic tile was thus exposed, affording more room for decorative flourishes.

The immediate acceptance of the Cronstedt-Wrede stove created a boom for the country's ceramic factories and another opportunity for the Swedes to demonstrate how the most functional objects can also be beautiful. The undisputed star of the field was the Marieberg

Tiled stoves were generally fashioned in either a cylindrical or a rectangular form with the top half sized slightly smaller than the base and delineated with a shelf.

RIGHT: Milky white glazed tiles decorated with a light touch have timeless appeal. OPPOSITE TOP, LEFT TO RIGHT: A recently built stove features unglazed tiles. An unusual pairing of a cylindrical top and a rectangular base. Carl Johan Cronstedt's great-great-grandson Jacob Cronstedt designed this stove, which also functions as a hot water heater via a concealed tank and offers a vented barbecue facing into the kitchen. OPPOSITE BOTTOM: An 18th-century stove featuring a repeating floral motif.

A SWEDISH STOVE IS NOT OUT OF THE QUESTION FOR AN AMERICAN HOUSE, SINCE ITS HEFT BELIES ITS MOBILITY. WHEN DRENCHED WITH WATER, THE GROUT BETWEEN THE TILES DISSOLVES AND THE STOVE CAN THEN BE DISMANTLED, PACKED IN A BOX, SHIPPED TO A NEW LOCATION, AND REGROUTED UPON REASSEMBLY. (SEE SOURCES.)

faience factory, which made brilliant white tiles bearing delicate, brightly colored motifs such as ribbons, bouquets, and classical urns and garlands.

Because brick and tile are modular, the stoves could assume a number of shapes. They could be boxlike or columnar; some were box-shaped and topped by a column. Some had beveled corners. Most were constructed with a shelf or a depression for a candle. During the Gustavian era, when symmetry prevailed in design, people often purchased a pair of stoves for a room, one a working model and the other a trompe l'oeil replica, painted to mimic its ceramic twin.

Many modern Swedish stoves still take their cue from their 18th-century precursors. Cronstedt's great-great-grandson, architect Jacob Cronstedt, created a stucco-covered stove for his country house that incorporates a hot water tank, a wood-burning grill, and a cubbyhole for storing logs.

IN PRAISE OF THE 18TH CENTURY

The brilliance of the 18th-century Swedish spirit came from an unusual combination of two traits: refinement and self-reliance. Two hundred years later the spirit pulses still, embodied in people like Lars Sjöberg, an art historian and curator at Stockholm's National Museum. Like many in his native land, Sjöberg is a cultured man who deeply appreciates beauty, values intellectual acuity —and wouldn't think of calling a handyman to repair a chair or repaint the house. At Odenslunda, the family home just north of Stockholm that he shares with his wife, Ursula, he is likely to be found up on a ladder, dressed in paint-spattered trousers and scraping an old wooden doorway.

Sjöberg's passion for the lessons of the 18th century runs so deep that he has become a virtual spokesman for the epoch, reminding Swedes of the glory of their past and imploring them to reconnect with the common-

Lars Sjöberg is a hands-on historian. He personally does the restoration work in his own home. RIGHT: His dining room is decorated in Gustavian style; the chairs are a seamless blend of antique and reproduction.

sense approaches to daily living that have proven their worth over two centuries. Stories about Sjöberg's near-missionary zeal for rescuing historic dwellings from certain demise serve to both inspire and entertain those in decorative art circles. He collects decaying manor houses the way others might take in birds with broken wings, hoping to nourish them back to health, and camps out for weeks in unheated houses while he restores them. "I finally had to set up a separate budget for the house," laughs Ursula, a curator of fine art at the prestigious Bukowski's auction house in Stockholm. "Otherwise he'd spend every penny we have restoring the houses, and our family would have nothing to eat!"

What no one would fault Sjöberg for is his encyclopedic knowledge of Swedish and European art history. His discourses are made delightful by the insertion of modern-day references to clarify his points. "Take the real creator of the Swedish Baroque, Queen Hedvig Eleonora," he says, referring to the first Swede to interpret classical Roman design, more than one hundred years before Gustav III. "She was a sort of architectural Margaret Thatcher, ruling the aesthetic development of Sweden with an iron fist! Few people realize

how directly Sweden was connected to classical influences. They think everything was first filtered through France. But Queen Hedvig Eleonora was putting statues of Apollo in the entrance of Drottningholm castle as early as the 1670s. By the mid-17th century Swedes were already developing Palladio's concept of the villa. Certainly we were influenced by the French, but I think we were even more classical than the French."

Sjöberg is most insistent, however, when extolling the values of the 18th century. "Sweden was in a position of having to rebuild after the long war with Russia.

We were able to create a strong connection between all levels of society—a true solidarity. We were guided by the Lutheran ideals of being clean, hardworking, honest, and responsible to one's community, with the well-off sharing the burdens of the common man. What is more, there was a level of artistic quality that went directly from the nobility down to the rural people."

Sjöberg doesn't lack for evidence to substantiate his beliefs. Pointing out a Gustavian chair placed against the wall, he elaborates on the quality of craftsmanship that characterized Swedish furniture

Perhaps the true charm of Sjöberg's home springs from his insistence that each object need not be cosmetically perfect, but rather should be allowed to show its age gracefully. TOP LEFT: The checked roller blinds are reproductions of 18th-century models. ABOVE: The front sitting room is simply furnished. RIGHT: A vasellier houses a collection of ceramic plates.

making in the 18th century. "We made things that made sense: If you can craft a chair two hundred years ago and it still works today, it must be a good design. Any individual part of this chair can be repaired separately. The seat pulls away from the frame so that it can easily be recovered when the cloth wears out. It bothers me when a fancy piece of furniture that needs one little thing repaired must be taken apart totally."

To help others from falling into this trap, Sjöberg has involved himself in a number of projects that not only help to educate Swedes about the past but also provide opportunities for the designs of 18th-century furniture to go back into production. In 1994, he was involved in the construction of Sjörby House, temporarily situated on the grounds outside the National Museum. Students participated in the construction, following the techniques of framing and woodcrafting typical of the late 18th century. He has also worked with the Swedish Board of National Antiquities to ensure that reproductions of 18th-century furnishings and accessories being produced by IKEA are as authentic as possible. Lastly, Sjöberg and Ursula have coauthored two books, one on Swedish chairs, and an excellent reference work on classic Swedish interiors entitled *The Swedish Room*.

For the moment, the 18th century seems very much alive.

THE
KITCHEN

"FOR SWEDISH FAMILIES, togetherness starts in the kitchen," says Gunilla von Arbin, the wife of the Swedish consul general in New York, Dag Sebastian Ahlander. "That is where we gather, where the kids do their homework, where we share the news of the day, and make our plans for the day to come. The kitchen really is the most important room in the house."

It is also one of the largest rooms. The narrow, galley-style "convenience

A Swedish kitchen provides a warm and cheery gathering place for all the family members.

kitchen" that became a fixture in so many postwar societies was roundly rejected in Sweden. This center of family life had always been a big yet cozy place—and a big, cozy place it would stay.

THE **BEST** ROOM

In the 1930s, the Swedish government undertook the Million Home Program, a monumental effort to build clean, affordable housing for working-class families. In a move reflective of the nation's cultural values, the "best room" in the prototypical new house was not the living room but rather the kitchen. Today, Swedes continue to prioritize the kitchen as the room on which to invest time, effort, and love.

First and foremost, the kitchen is centered with a table large enough to accommodate everyone in the family, for it is here and not in the dining room where most meals are served. Considered a friendlier and more inviting spot, the kitchen is used not only for family dining but to receive close friends as well.

This intimacy can be clearly seen in the flow of an elegant dinner party, according to Dag Sebastian Ahlander. The evening begins with a formal dinner graciously served in the dining room. Coffee, dessert, and the approach of midnight bring to a close much of the visiting, and guests begin to take their leave. Then, somewhere between 12:30 and 1:00 A.M., a small lingering band of friends find their way to the kitchen where the *nattsexa*—a light supper consisting perhaps of a nightcap and *pyttipanna*, a tasty hash of pota-

KITCHEN CABINETS CAN BE GIVEN A FACELIFT AND A SWEDISH ACCENT WITH A STROKE OF THE PAINTBRUSH. FOR A FRESH AND INVITING LOOK CONSIDER PAINTING THEM IN A PALE BLUE. WHILE YOU ARE AT IT, WHY NOT MIX YOUR OWN EGG TEMPERA PAINT (SEE RECIPE, PAGE 176). APPLIED IN SEVERAL THIN COATS, TEMPERA PAINTS YIELD A STURDY YET DELICATELY LUMINOUS SURFACE. THE PAINT WILL DEVELOP A SOFT PATINA OVER TIME, AND SHOULD RESIST CHIPPING AROUND KNOBS AND HANDLES.

OPPOSITE: Through a quarter of a century and five children, the kitchen of Marie-Louise and Daniel Bonnier has changed very little. A large wooden table welcomes one and all, blue cabinets recall the sea just outside, and wooden floors grow more beautiful with each passing year. ABOVE: Nothing is more quintessentially Swedish than a lamp suspended over the center of the kitchen table.

OPPOSITE: The lamp centered over the Stackelbergs' kitchen table is cleverly constructed from a pewter pitcher. Note the crispbread drying on the poles suspended from the ceiling. BELOW: Wood is the preferred material for kitchen countertops.

toes and beef or salmon topped with a fried egg—will be shared along with stories and laughter. The *nattsexa* is considered the glory of the evening, a gift of friendship. And it is to the kitchen, and no other spot in the house, that friends will always turn as the venue for these intimate gatherings.

Perhaps the most appealing characteristic of the Swedish kitchen is its cheery atmosphere. Large windows let in maximum light; warm woods, often painted in engaging hues of blue, further enhance the bright mood; and an enchanting array of knickknacks, houseplants, kitchen tools, and the ever-present candles completes the homey and inviting scene. Attention to this sort of detail will make any kitchen a strong magnet for family members, providing a gentle counterweight to all the modern influences that can draw us apart.

A charming and nearly universal feature of Swedish kitchens is the lamp suspended above the table. For many years this lamp took the form of an inverted bowl covered with a cloth shade that was trimmed around the bottom edge with a ruffle (like the lamp shown on page 106). It was inspired by the lamp artist Carl Larsson hung over the table in his own kitchen, which became so endeared to the Swedes that they took to calling it the "Larsson lamp." In recent years, however, a variety of shades have become available, made not only of cloth but also of parchment, thin sculpted metal, or glass. Attractive and practical, the lamps provide good task lighting for the many hours of the day when the kitchen table serves as desk and work or hobby surface.

Finally, no Swedish kitchen would be complete without at least one striped cotton rag runner, invariably including at least one shade of blue! Used most often in front of the sink, where the sturdy fabric can wick up any splashes, rag runners can also be found in any high traffic area in the room.

STORAGE AND DISPLAY

If one thinks of the Swedish kitchen as a symphony in wood, the crescendo is reached in its practical and graceful wooden accoutrements: spatulas, spoons, butter knives, bowls, countertops, and more are all made from this practical and accommodating material. But it is perhaps the many wooden shelves, racks, and ledges dotting the walls that give the kitchen its particular charm.

The brilliance of Swedish storage and display systems lies in their clever designs and the use of affordable materials. These devices can easily be adapted to any kitchen, and constructed or installed by most do-it-yourselfers. Supplementing the storage space offered by cabinets are various configurations of shelves and racks. For example, a notched and beveled strip of wood serves as a hanging rack for mixing spoons; a curved plank surrounding the hood of the stove doubles as a display shelf for carved wooden horses; a set of shallow planks resting upon scroll brackets performs the role of spice rack. Variations on the theme of storage and display are as endless as the supply of lumber, and all add to the warm and personal atmosphere of the room.

OPPOSITE AND TOP RIGHT: In the home built by his late father Carl, Egil Malmsten carefully maintains the ingenious and attractive collections of carved wooden utensils, storage racks, and shelves. LEFT AND TOP LEFT: Nooks and crannies abound in Swedish kitchens, serving purposes both decorative and functional.

THE
TABLE

SWEDISH CUISINE, WHILE not as well known internationally as its French or Italian counterparts, can be every bit as sumptuous and refined. From delicately poached salmon, to boiled new potatoes topped with a dollop of cream and crowned with caviar, to exquisite lingonberry tarts, Sweden offers a wide range of fresh, healthy, and flavorful menus for entertaining as well as everyday fare.

An especially appealing aspect of

Working from an 18th-century recipe, Lovisa Tenglin made this torte in the wood-burning ovens of Skogaholm, the Gustavian manor on the grounds of the Skansen open-air museum.

Sweden's food culture is *husmanskost* or home cooking. Hearty time-honored classics such as Swedish meatballs or stuffed cabbage rolls are still prepared in homes all over the country, and offer delicious options for your own family dinners.

S K Å L ! —
TO THE SPIRIT
OF SWEDEN

Few customs so delightfully start off any gathering on a convivial note as the first toast—or *skål*—offered by the host. The glasses are always filled with aquavit, the cherished drink at the heart of every Swedish celebration. Aquavit begins its life as a simple vodka and then is flavored with aromatic herbs, fruits, or spices to become one of the spunkiest drinks ever to grace a table.

The practice of flavoring vodka originated not as a search for something festive or exotic but rather as a method of disguising its unpleasant taste. For centuries, Swedes in the southern provinces distilled a primitive type of vodka known as *brännvin*, or "burned wine," from grains or potatoes; they then "purified" the liquid by running it through charcoal. The resulting flavor was perfectly vile. To render the drink palatable, the Swedes gathered locally grown herbs and spices, such as caraway, anise, and fennel, and let them soak in the spirits for a number of days. When enough flavor had been released into the *brännvin* to mask the taste, it was ready to drink.

OPPOSITE: Summer sunlight dances off the ice-cloaked bottle of aquavit on Louise Carling's sideboard. ABOVE: An elegant collection of 18th-century schnapps glasses designed in the traditional trumpet shape.

TO CREATE A PRETTY PRESENTATION FOR GUESTS, PLACE A SCHNAPPS BOTTLE INSIDE A SLIGHTLY LARGER PLASTIC CONTAINER—A HALF-GALLON MILK CARTON WORKS PERFECTLY. FOR DECORATION, SLIDE BLOSSOMS, WHOLE FLOWERS WITH STEMS, BERRIES, SPRIGS OF MINT, OR SLICES OF FRUIT INTO THE NARROW SPACE BETWEEN THE BOTTLE AND CONTAINER, TAKING CARE TO STACK THEM EVENLY AROUND THE BOTTLE. POUR WATER INTO THE SPACE, FILLING TO ABOUT AN INCH FROM THE BOTTLE TOP, AND PLACE THE CONTAINER IN THE FREEZER. ONCE ICE FORMS AROUND THE BOTTLE, YOU CAN REMOVE THE CONTAINER FROM THE FREEZER AND RINSE WITH WARM WATER SO THE PLASTIC CONTAINER WILL SLIP OFF THE ICE. PRESENT THE ICE-CLOAKED BOTTLE ON A TRAY DECORATED WITH MORE HERBS OR FLOWERS.

Schnapps, or aquavit, is often flavored. Herbs and spices are allowed to soak for several days, releasing their flavors into the vodka. Regarding the etiquette of drinking schnapps: The first toast is always offered by the host; only then can other guests follow suit. A *skål* is generally addressed to someone in particular. Both people maintain eye contact as they take the first sip of their drinks.

Today the vodka produced in Sweden is completely pure. In fact, Sweden's best-known vodka, Absolut, was born with the full name *Absolut Rent Brännvin*, to advertise the fact that it was absolutely pure burned wine. A variety of flavors, however, continue to be added to create tasty aquavits. Although many versions of flavored vodka are available commercially, such as Herrgåd, a cumin-flavored variety hailing from the south of Sweden, or Absolut's citron or black currant vodkas, most Swedes have a favorite recipe or two for creating their own homemade schnapps with a pure vodka base. (The term "schnapps" has become a synonym for aquavit, but it actually refers to the trumpet-shaped shot glass in which aquavit is traditionally served.)

To make schnapps, one starts with vodka, then adds raspberry, lemon, black currant, or any of a host of other flavors (see Recipes). The ingredients soak in the vodka anywhere from three days to a week, depending upon the quantity added to the liquid and the desired taste of the final spirit. After the flavors have been released into the vodka, the liquid is strained and returned to the bottle.

Traditionally the first toast of aquavit took place around a "schnapps table," a beautifully decorated occasional table or sideboard featuring a small assortment of savory hors d'oeuvres and crispbreads. According to Swedish folklore expert Jan-Öjvind Swahn, the custom traces its roots to the 18th century, when upper-class Swedes took a fancy to the Russian practice of starting off a meal with a cou-

ple of shots of vodka and some smoked fish. With time, this ritual became increasingly extravagant and blossomed into an immense *smörgåsbord* (*smörgås* means sandwich and *bord* means table) consisting of a sumptuous variety of cold and hot dishes. The full-fledged smorgasbord eventually became too cumbersome for home entertaining and moved into the domain of restaurateurs. Today, smorgasbords are generally offered only during the Christmas season.

Many wonderful elements of the old traditional schnapps table and smorgasbord have evolved into new customs that suit modern home entertaining. The host will create a special moment at the beginning of a dinner for the first toast of aquavit. Leading everyone in singing a *snapsvisa*, or schnapps song, he follows with warm words of welcome specially chosen for the guests and the occasion. This initial glass of aquavit is served with a scaled-down smorgasbord, often presented on a beautifully set sideboard. Guests raise their glasses, help themselves to their favorite dishes, and seat themselves at the table. Among the delectable hors d'oeuvres might be *matjessill*, a sweet pickled herring; different preparations of Swedish caviar, such as bleak roe and red onion on cucumber segments, or bleak roe in small baked potatoes; and, of course, salmon, either smoked, marinated, or poached. All are offered with *knäckebröd*, Swedish crispbread lathered with creamy butter.

THE SWEDISH
CHEF

Chef Christer Larsson brings his native specialties to New York City at his West Side restaurant.

Fifteen years ago, after a decade spent mastering his craft, chef Christer Larsson decided to see if he could build a following for his native cuisine among Americans. Well aware that Swedish cuisine was all but unknown in this country, Larsson believed that the classic, healthy dishes that comprised his repertoire could find a following. After working in Atlanta, Los Angeles, and the resort town of Hilton Head, South Carolina, he landed his first major position in 1985 as executive chef at Aquavit, a posh Scandinavian restaurant in Manhattan. Larsson built such a strong reputation there that eight years later he opened Christer's, a more relaxed but equally successful restaurant specializing in Swedish dishes.

For all the endless hours Larsson has dedicated to the mastery of fine restaurant cuisine, he remains particularly fond of the traditional Swedish foods that are prepared in the home and believes they hold strong appeal for the American home cook as well.

C.M.: *How do you describe Swedish home cooking?*

C.L.: Home cooking is the kind of food I ate as a boy and the food my sons want me to prepare today. It's good, healthy cooking: Swedish meatballs, cabbage rolls, poached salmon—things like that. And everything with potatoes! Potatoes are indisputably the foundation of every meal in Sweden. When my mom hadn't yet decided what she would prepare for dinner, she would say, "Well, you start peeling the potatoes and I'll go figure out what we'll have tonight!"

Dill is also used very commonly in Sweden. Everyone always has a little bunch of dill in the refrigerator, and it is sold in the markets with the roots still attached, so it lasts longer. Many people place dill in the water when they boil potatoes. The thicker stems can go in the pot and then the cooked potatoes get served with little bits of the feathery tops.

Swedish home cooking lends itself well to American kitchens. The ingredients are affordable, easy to find, and easy to work with—we rely on root vegetables, ground meat, and fish.

C.M.: *Many Americans are a little intimidated by cooking fish. We're never sure how to prepare it, how long to cook it, how to check to see if it's done. What advice can you offer?*

C.L.: Stay with it! Fish is easier and faster to cook than meat, and it is much easier to digest. To prepare meat well, you have to marinate it and put some effort into seasoning it. With fish, just squeeze on a little lemon juice, cook ten minutes—and it's great. Of course, like anything you cook in the home, baking fish takes a little experience. There really aren't any rules, because people's ovens vary, as does the thickness of the fish. Just experiment a little. Bake the fish for fifteen minutes, then taste it . . . see what you like and make your adjustments. I always press the fish with my finger; if it resists slightly, I know it is done the way I like it. After a while you will get to know what degree of firmness corresponds to the level at which you prefer your fish to be cooked.

Poaching is another great example of why fish is so "user friendly," since it offers you quite a bit of flexibility to accommodate whatever is going on in your kitchen. You can put the fish in your poaching liquid for about five minutes, take it out, let it relax for a while. The juices will spread out and the fish will stay nice and moist. Then, if too much time goes by and you want to warm the fish back up, you can put it back in the water for a couple of minutes to reheat it. It's not going to ruin the fish.

And remember to experiment with spices. Try lemon, dill, ginger, or any other spice you particularly like. Discover what your family prefers. This is the key to home cooking—putting your soul into it, the little touch of love for your family.

C.M.: *What are favorite dishes for newcomers to Swedish food?*

C.L.: I find that Americans love to try the herring dishes and smoked salmon dishes. In general Americans are very open to all Swedish cuisine. The only reluctance I notice is to receiving a whole fish, head, tail, and bones included. In Sweden we are accustomed to taking our fish off the bone on our plate. A little bone or two remaining in a sardine or herring doesn't really cause us any trouble. We feel it just adds a tiny crunch!

C.M.: *What about the composition of the meal—what types of food do you put together and what beverages do you serve to accompany the food?*

C.L.: It is important not to overload the tastebuds. As a rule of thumb, we present no more than three flavors on the plate—for example, a poached fish, potatoes, and a vegetable. If you crowd too much on the plate, it becomes more difficult to appreciate the essential qualities of the food you are serving. With regard to the beverages accompanying the meal, we have some long-established traditions. Schnapps—a drink with a lot of character—accompanies the robustly flavored appetizers, dishes that are cured or pickled with sugar, salt, or vinegar. With the main course, we serve a nice Swedish beer, because its taste complements the food. Of course at lunch, people will more often choose Ramlösa, our spring water, or a light version of the beer.

About **Salmon**

Salmon is a favorite fish in Sweden. Although it slightly trails the herring in the quantity consumed in Swedish homes, salmon offers the American home cook the surest route into the fresh, healthy dishes that typify Swedish cuisine.

Even if the salmon wasn't so delicious, it's hard not to stand in awe of these beautiful creatures for navigating the demanding lives foisted upon them by Mother Nature. Imagine having to swim as many as one thousand danger-laden miles from your freshwater birthplace to the ocean only to retrace the same harrowing path several years later. Any salmon that survives gets to mate and then die of exhaustion—thus bequeathing its legacy to a new school of youngsters.

PURCHASING FRESH SALMON

As with purchasing any fresh fish, it is wise to rely upon the expertise and counsel of a good fishmonger. Many "all-purpose" supermarkets don't turn over enough fresh fish to maintain proper standards, so they resort to selling only frozen fish, or offer lesser-quality specimens wrapped tightly in plastic to veil any unpleasant odors. The salmon you choose—be it whole, filleted, or cut into steaks—should boast shiny skin, firm pink flesh that clings tightly to the bone, and a mild, pleasant odor. Don't accept any product that reveals brown edges or gills. When purchasing a whole fish, look for protruding eyes that shine bright and clear. The color of the flesh will vary by

the species: West Coast salmon, such as chinook or coho, will be darker pink than Atlantic salmon, such as Nova Scotia or Norwegian salmon. Salmon caught in the wild will be slightly thicker in the tail region than farm-raised salmon, because of the muscular activity required to swim upstream.

When you arrive home with your salmon, run the fish under cold water, then pat it dry with a paper towel. Salmon can be prepared immediately or can be wrapped tightly in plastic and stored in the refrigerator for no more than two days. Salmon is also delicious cooked and then served cold.

GRAVLAX

In Swedish, *grav* means grave and *lax* means salmon. The history behind the name bears witness to the good instincts of 14th-century Swedes. During the spring—the best time to fish for salmon—waterlogged soil and the lack of adequate paths made the transport of the catch all but impossible for the fishermen of the Middle Ages. It was equally impossible for them to afford or carry enough salt to properly preserve their catch.

The solution, instead, was to bury the fish in a trench lined with birch bark. Just enough salt was added to start the fermentation process, then a few stones and logs were laid over the "grave" to keep wild animals at bay. Six months later, when the ground froze again and could support the weight of their sleds, the fishermen returned to dig up their *gravlax*.

Today, gravlax remains a favorite delicacy, though the salmon is obviously no longer fermented in trenches! Home cooks often cure their fresh salmon fillets in a mixture of kosher salt, dill sprigs, sugar, and aquavit. More often than not, however, ready-to-eat gravlax is purchased at a favorite market.

SMOKED SALMON

The best smoked salmon is extremely delicate and not at all salty. Highly prized Nova Scotia smoked salmon, which comes from the Maritime Provinces of eastern Canada, is considered to be the most buttery in texture. Nova Scotia salmon should always be sliced thinly and on the diagonal. Scottish, Irish, and Norwegian cold-smoked salmon are also superb varieties; these have a slightly drier texture. Smoked salmon, available in vacuum packs through mail-order houses such as Ducktrap Farms (see Sources), makes a delicious treat for special dinners or brunches.

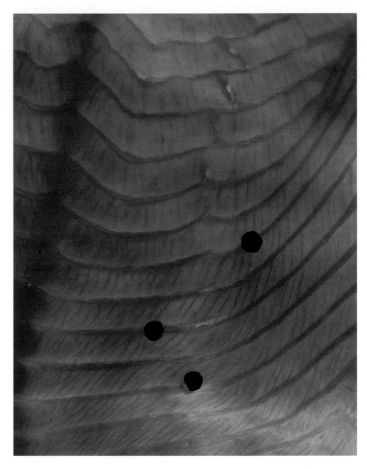

BAKING, GRILLING, OR POACHING FRESH SALMON

Salmon is a very easy, and very quick, fish to prepare. Even the novice home cook can create an impressive and crowd-pleasing dish. Recipes for poached and baked salmon can be found in The Resource Guide (page 174). With any of these methods, the fish should be cooked to your liking. Some people cook salmon until the flesh flakes easily; others consider flaky salmon to be overcooked. As a general rule, as soon as the flesh turns opaque (place a knife into the flesh to check), it can be eaten.

WASTE NOT, WANT NOT

According to Ulrika Bengtsson, the resident chef at the Swedish consul general's residence in New York City, one of the salmon's greatest virtues is its complete "usability." It is not at all fragile, thus nothing is likely to be lost in the preparation. Bones make great fish stock, salmon roe is a delicacy, and even leftovers, combined with sour cream in a food processor, can be transformed into a mousse, a true party treat.

A TALE OF TWO DINNERS

Chef Christer Larsson has prepared two dinners, each comprising three courses, that can easily be prepared by the home cook. The main courses, Swedish meat-balls and poached salmon, are traditional favorites that are sure to win acceptance at your table. (See "Classic Swedish Meals," page 172.)

TOP, LEFT TO RIGHT: The meal begins with "Gentlemen's Delight," a tantalizing mixture of two Swedish delicacies—smoked roe and her-ring—plus a blend of fresh herbs and chopped hard-boiled egg. (Smoked roe is sold in tubes and can be found wherever Scandinavian foods are sold.) Practically synonymous with Sweden, meat-balls are a favorite dinner and every family has their own special version of the traditional recipe. Christer underlines the importance of using the leanest beef possible. Lingonberries and cucum-ber salad provide the perfect counterpoint to the main dish. Berries of all sorts figure prominently in Swedish desserts. Here, Christer has combined blueberries and strawberries and molded them with brioche. A dollop of lemon sabayon is added on the top.

BOTTOM, LEFT TO RIGHT: Winter meals often begin with a soul-comforting bowl of hot soup. Here, a traditional combination of cabbage and home-made chicken broth begins the meal. Salmon is a staple in Sweden and is most often simply pre-pared in a poaching liquid seasoned with root vegetables and herbs. Fresh dill sprigs are always used for garnish. Little crêpes called *plättar* are a traditional dessert in Sweden. Nothing can equal the combination of lingonberry preserves and vanilla ice cream as a topping. Christer makes the crêpes ahead of time and simply reheats them before bringing them to the table.

SUMPTUOUS BERRIES

Come September, the Swedish woods beckon with a bounty of "red gold," the round, ruby-colored, slightly sweet, slightly tart lingonberries that lend a rosy cast to the landscape. Families stroll with baskets on their arms, always at the ready to harvest this versatile fruit. Most of the lingonberries are preserved as jam and enjoyed throughout the year, not only with pancakes and waffles but also with meat dishes and as filling for dessert puddings. Fresh lingonberries make a delicious treat simply served in a bowl with some milk or crème fraîche. And, pressed for its juice, the lingonberry makes a very refreshing drink.

While fresh lingonberries are hard to come by in the United States, lingonberry jam is widely available through mail-order catalogs and at IKEA superstores (see Sources). Chef Ulrika Bengtsson uses the preserves to make a sumptuous multi-tiered dessert, alternating thin Swedish crêpes with sweet jam (see Recipes), while chef Christer Larsson believes berry preserves to be the perfect counterpoint to traditional Swedish meatballs. In your own kitchen, you'll discover any number of ways to enjoy this Swedish treat.

LEFT: Gathering lingonberries is a fall institution in the forests of Sweden. The famous red berries are enjoyed fresh as well as preserved in jams to provide a steady supply until the next harvest. ABOVE: All types of summer berries are pressed for refreshing drinks.

LINGONBERRY SORBET
8 ounces lingonberry preserves
1/3 cup sugar
1 cup simple syrup (dissolve 1/2 part
sugar to 1 part water)
1 egg white, lightly whipped
(alternative)

Mix the preserves and sugar in a saucepan. Bring it to a boil over medium heat, then remove and let cool slightly. Add the simple syrup, pour the mixture into a blender, and mix. Pour it into an ice cream maker and follow manufacturer's instructions.

Alternatively, place the mixture in the freezer. When it is just beginning to crystallize, mix in the egg white.

Serve as is, or with fresh fruit.

THE RESOURCE GUIDE

CLASSIC SWEDISH MEALS

CHRISTER LARSSON'S SWEDISH MEATBALL DINNER
(SERVES FOUR)

GENTLEMEN'S DELIGHT ■ SWEDISH MEATBALLS WITH
LINGONBERRIES AND CUCUMBER SALAD
BLUEBERRY BRIOCHE PUDDING WITH LEMON SABAYON

GENTLEMEN'S DELIGHT

4 hard-boiled eggs, chopped
½ medium red onion, chopped
2 ounces smoked cod roe, or
    1 tablespoon sour cream
2 sprigs dill, chopped
¼ bunch chives, chopped (about 2
    tablespoons)
2 herring fillets, chopped
Pumpernickel bread, thinly sliced, or
    Swedish crispbread, for serving
Dill sprigs for garnish

Place the first six ingredients in a bowl and mix to make a paste. Spread on pumpernickel or crispbread. Serve on small plates garnished with a sprig of dill. (See Sources for specialty ingredients.)

SWEDISH MEATBALLS WITH LINGONBERRIES AND CUCUMBER SALAD

In Sweden, lingonberry preserves are often served to enhance a main dish. They are available in the United States at gourmet markets or by mail order (see Sources).

CUCUMBER SALAD

1 medium cucumber
4 tablespoons distilled white vinegar
6 tablespoons sugar
½ cup water
Chopped parsley, for garnish

Cut the cucumber into thin slices. Combine the vinegar, sugar, and water in a saucepan and bring to a boil, then remove from the heat and allow to cool.

Place the cucumber slices in a glass bowl or other nonreactive bowl. Cover with the vinegar mixture and allow to marinate for 2 hours.

When ready to serve with meatballs, remove the cucumber slices from the marinating liquid with a slotted spoon. Serve a small portion and garnish with chopped parsley.

MEATBALLS

1 medium red onion, finely chopped
3 tablespoons butter
1 pound very lean ground beef
1 medium potato, peeled, boiled,
    chilled, and grated
1 egg, lightly beaten
2 teaspoons salt
Freshly ground pepper to taste
¼ teaspoon ground allspice
1 cup lingonberry preserves

Sauté the onion over medium heat in 1 tablespoon of the butter. Remove to a plate and allow to cool in the refrigerator.

Combine the ground beef, chopped onion, grated potato, and egg. Season with salt, pepper, and allspice. Roll the mixture into small balls about 1 inch in diameter. Melt the remaining 2 tablespoons of butter in a heavy skillet over medium-high heat; add the meatballs in batches and sauté until golden brown, about 4 to 5 minutes. Remove the first batches to a warm oven until all the meatballs have been cooked.

Divide the meatballs among 4 plates, garnish each with a tablespoon or two of lingonberry preserves, and serve with Cucumber Salad.

BLUEBERRY BRIOCHE PUDDING WITH LEMON SABAYON

BRIOCHE PUDDING

2 cups fresh or frozen blueberries
1 cup strawberries, quartered
½ cup sugar
¼ teaspoon ground cardamom
1 medium loaf brioche bread

LEMON SABAYON

Zest and juice of 1 lemon
3 tablespoons sugar
3 tablespoons water
1 cup heavy cream
3 egg yolks

To make the Brioche Pudding: Place the blueberries, strawberries, sugar, and cardamom in a saucepan and bring to a boil. Reduce the heat and let simmer for 15 minutes. The berries will release their juices to create a jamlike consistency. Remove from heat.

Meanwhile, cut the brioche loaf into cubes 1 inch square and divide into four small molds or cups. Top with the berry mixture to saturate

cubes. Place molds in the refrigerator for 30 minutes to set.

To make the Lemon Sabayon: Bring the lemon zest, lemon juice, sugar, and water to a boil. Cook over high heat to reduce to a thick syrup. Let the syrup cool. In a bowl, lightly beat the cream and set aside. Place the egg yolks in a stainless steel

bowl and add the lemon syrup. Place the bowl over a pot of boiling water and whisk it constantly until the egg mixture turns into a thick foam. Fold the cream into the egg mixture, then strain it through a sieve.

Unmold each pudding and serve topped with the Lemon Sabayon.

CHRISTER LARSSON'S SALMON DINNER

(SERVES FOUR)

SAVOY CABBAGE SOUP ▪ POACHED SALMON WITH DILL SAUCE
SWEDISH PANCAKES WITH LINGONBERRIES AND ICE CREAM

SAVOY CABBAGE SOUP

Roasting a whole chicken is worth the extra effort, since you not only have a delicious soup for dinner but can also treat yourself to roasted chicken breast salad the following day.

1 roasting chicken, 3 to 4 pounds
Melted butter
1 leek
1 carrot, peeled and cut into 2-inch
  pieces
1 medium yellow onion, coarsely
  chopped
2 stalks celery
2 bay leaves
1 teaspoon black peppercorns
6 allspice berries
4 garlic cloves
1 sprig thyme
2½ quarts water
2 tablespoons butter
1 pound savoy cabbage, finely
  shredded
Salt and pepper to taste
½ bunch fresh dill, chopped, for gar-
  nish (about ¼ cup)

Preheat the oven to 350° F. Brush the surface of the chicken with melted butter. Place the chicken on a rack in a roasting pan, breast down. Roast for approximately 1 hour, turning it after 30 minutes and cooking until golden brown.

Strip the breast meat from the chicken (leaving a little bit of meat on the bones to add more flavor to the stock) and reserve for another use. Also remove about ¾ of the leg meat. Tear into small chunks and

reserve to add to the finished soup.

Trim the roots off the bottom of the leek and cut the green tops off to about 2 inches from the white stock. Cut the leek in half lengthwise, then rinse thoroughly under running water to remove any sand. Cut each half into 1-inch pieces.

Place the chicken carcass in a large, deep, heavy-bottomed pot and add the leek, carrot, onion, celery, spices, and water. Bring to a boil, then lower the heat and simmer for 1½ hours. Strain the stock, discarding vegetables, and skim it to remove the fat.

Meanwhile, melt the 2 tablespoons of butter in a heavy pot and brown the cabbage for about 15 minutes over medium heat. Add the stock and let simmer over medium heat for another 25 to 30 minutes, adding extra water if a thinner broth is desired.

Season the soup with salt and freshly ground pepper. Add the reserved chunks of leg meat and heat through, about 5 minutes.

Serve in soup bowls sprinkled with fresh chopped dill.

POACHED SALMON
WITH DILL SAUCE

SAUCE

1 shallot, chopped
½ cup dry white wine
1 sprig fresh thyme or ½ teaspoon dried
12 black peppercorns
1 cup bottled clam juice
½ cup heavy cream
Salt and pepper to taste
½ bunch dill, chopped

SALMON

2 pounds salmon fillet, with skin
1 leek
1 carrot, peeled and sliced
1 medium red onion, sliced
2 quarts water
½ cup distilled vinegar
12 allspice berries
1 tablespoon black peppercorns
Dill sprigs for garnish

To make the sauce: Place the shallot in a saucepan with the wine, thyme, and peppercorns. Bring to a boil over high heat and reduce the liquid by half. Add clam juice and cream, lower the heat, and simmer for 5 to 8 minutes. Strain through a sieve and season. Add the chopped dill just before serving. The sauce can be made before the salmon is poached, and kept warm.

To prepare the salmon: Cut the fillet into four equal portions, leaving the skin on. Trim the roots off the bottom of the leek and cut the green tops off to about 2 inches from the white stock. Cut the leek in half lengthwise, then rinse thoroughly under running water to remove sand. Cut into 1-inch pieces.

Place the carrot, onion, and leek in a heavy pot with the water, vinegar, allspice, and peppercorns. Bring to a boil and add salmon. Return to a boil and simmer for 6 to 8 minutes, until salmon is fully opaque. It should still be a little soft inside.

Using a slotted spoon, remove the salmon from the poaching liquid and place on plates. Garnish with the vegetables used in poaching and with sprigs of dill. Top each fillet with sauce. Serve with boiled new potatoes with their skins left on.

SWEDISH PANCAKES
WITH LINGONBERRIES AND
ICE CREAM

Plättar, as they are called, are a traditional dessert. The pancakes can be made ahead, but should then be reheated at the last moment so they are brought to the table warm.

2 eggs
1¼ cups flour
3 cups milk
2 tablespoons unsalted butter, melted, plus extra for brushing
½ teaspoon salt
4–6 tablespoons lingonberry preserves
Vanilla ice cream
Confectioners' sugar for garnish, optional

Heat the oven to warm. In a large bowl, whisk the eggs, flour, and a little of the milk to create a smooth paste. Add the rest of the milk, the melted butter, and the salt. Mix well.

Heat a heavy skillet* and brush lightly with the extra melted butter. Pour in the batter, forming small, thin pancakes about 1½ inches in diameter. Cook the pancakes over medium heat for about a minute on each side. This batter should be enough for 28 pancakes.

Using ovenproof plates, as pancakes are cooked, arrange each serving on a plate by placing six pancakes in a circle and a seventh in the center. Place in the oven to stay warm. Take care handling hot plates when removing.

To serve: Top each pancake with a large dollop of lingonberry preserves and a small scoop of ice cream. Dust with confectioners' sugar if desired. Bring to the table immediately and alert guests that plates are hot.

*A *plättagg,* which is a special cast-iron skillet used for making *plättar* (seen on page 169), is available through catalogs specializing in Swedish products (see Sources).

More of Chef Christer Larsson's specialties can be sampled at his restaurant: Christer's, 154 West 55 Street, New York, NY, 212-974-7224.

MORE RECIPES

BAKED SALMON WITH
TOASTED ALMONDS
(SERVES FOUR)

Chef Ulrika Bengtsson proposes this delightful combination of salmon with buttery toasted almonds accompanied by a classic dill potato salad. Serve her version of Swedish Pancake Torte for dessert.

24 ounces fresh salmon fillet
Salt and pepper
4 tablespoons butter, at room temperature
½ cup sliced almonds

Preheat oven to 450° F. Cut the salmon into four equal servings and season with salt and pepper. Allow to rest for 15 minutes, then place in a large ovenproof casserole. Spread butter evenly over the fish and cover with almond slices. Bake for 8 to 10 minutes, according to preference.

DILL POTATO SALAD

(SERVES FOUR)

*14 small new potatoes, boiled until
   just tender (don't overcook)*
Juice and zest of 1 lemon
2 tablespoons olive oil
Salt and white pepper to taste
3 tablespoons chopped fresh dill

Allow the potatoes to cool enough to handle. Slice while still warm and place in a serving bowl.

Whisk together the lemon juice, lemon zest, and oil. Season with salt and pepper. Pour the dressing over the potato slices and toss. Just before serving, add the chopped dill and toss lightly.

This salad can also be served cold, but don't add the dill until just before serving.

SWEDISH PANCAKE TORTE WITH LINGONBERRIES

(SERVES FOUR)

1 egg
½ cup all-purpose flour
1 tablespoon sugar
Pinch of salt
1 cup milk
1 cup heavy cream
½–1 cup lingonberry preserves

To make the Swedish pancakes: Place a glass or metal mixing bowl in the freezer for 10 minutes to chill.

Beat the egg, then whisk in the flour, sugar, and salt. Add the milk. Strain the batter if it is very lumpy, and let sit for 15 minutes.

Lightly oil and heat a griddle over medium heat. Pour the batter onto the hot griddle to make four thin crêpes about 7 inches in diameter. Cook about 1 minute on each side until they are a golden brown. Watch carefully not to overcook. When cooked, stack on an oven-proof plate and keep in a warm oven. Handle the hot plate carefully.

Place the heavy cream in the chilled mixing bowl, and whip using a hand mixer at high speed, until it forms stiff peaks.

Build a layered torte by alternating each crêpe with a thin layer of lingonberry preserves and a slightly thicker layer of whipped cream. Finish with a dollop of whipped cream on top and cut into four portions. Serve immediately.

SWEDISH PRUNE TORTE

(SERVES EIGHT)

Lovisa Tenglin of the Skansen Museum in Stockholm made this torte, shown on page 159, from an 18th-century recipe.

FILLING

1 pound prunes, pitted
½ pound dried figs
1½ cups white wine
*½–1 cup sugar, according to
   preference*
1 tablespoon ground cinnamon
*Peel of 1 large lemon, removed with a
   sharp vegetable peeler and cut into
   small slivers*

PASTRY

1 cup sugar
2 cups all-purpose flour
*16 tablespoons (2 sticks) unsalted
   butter, softened*
1 egg

GLAZE

½ cup confectioners' sugar
¼ teaspoon vanilla extract
2 teaspoons water

To make the filling: Cut the prunes in half and slice the figs into small pieces. Place the prunes in a heavy-bottomed pan; add just enough water to cover. Boil gently for 15 minutes, stir occasionally. Add figs and wine, continue cooking at a slow boil for 15 minutes, or until mixture reaches a marmalade-like consistency.

Begin adding the sugar, ¼ cup at a time to taste. Continue to boil gently for a few minutes, then add cinnamon and lemon peel. Turn off the heat, but wait 5 to 10 minutes before removing pan from stove. Set filling aside to cool.

To make the pastry: Preheat oven to 350° F. Sift together sugar and all but 2 tablespoons of flour. Work in butter and egg. If dough is too sticky, gradually add remaining flour until it is the consistency of sugar cookie dough.

Working with a quarter of the dough at a time, roll onto a sheet of lightly floured parchment to about ⅛-inch thick. Cut 2 rounds each of 3, 4, 6, and 9 inches diameter. Bake rounds on parchment-lined cooking sheets for about 10 minutes, or until golden. Remove to a cooling rack to cool.

When rounds are cool, spread the fruit filling evenly on one of each diameter. Make "filled cookies" by matching each round with its mate. Starting with the 9-inch round, stack the filled cookies on a serving dish, ending with the 3-inch round.

To make the glaze: Whisk confectioners' sugar, vanilla, and water in small bowl until smooth. Drizzle layered torte with glaze. To serve, cut with a sharp, serrated knife to prevent pastry from cracking.

NOTE: The Haram Christensen company supplies many food stores throughout the United States with Swedish specialties such as cod roe, Swedish anchovies, and herring. For retail locations, call (800) 937-3424.

PAINTING/COLOR PALETTE

PAINT RECIPES

Here are Ralph Edenheim's recipes:

EGG TEMPERA PAINT

1 egg
2 ounces boiled linseed oil
1 tablespoon water
1 tablespoon or more of powdered pig-
ment(s), according to preference

Mix the egg and oil together with a whisk. Mix in the 1 tablespoon of water. Add just enough water to the powdered pigment to make a smooth paste, then stir into the egg-oil mixture. This will make approximately enough paint to cover a side chair. Egg tempera can be stored up to three weeks if refrigerated in a tightly covered jar.

DISTEMPER PAINT

2½ quarts water
11 pounds chalk (sometimes called
whiting)
3½ ounces (200 grams) horn or bone
glue*
Dry pigment

Pour the water into a large bucket. Add the chalk—it will largely sit on top of water. Leave overnight to permit the water to absorb the chalk. In a second, smaller bucket, place the glue with just enough water to cover the surface. Leave overnight also.

The next day, place the bucket of glue on the stovetop over a larger pan containing simmering water. (You must use this double boiler method so as not to burn the glue.) Heat the glue slowly until it melts and is free of lumps. Then pour the warm glue into the chalk-and-water mixture and mix well until thoroughly blended. (This will take a little bit

of elbow grease.) Tint the mixture by dissolving powdered pigment in just enough water so that it liquifies; mix it into the distemper. Test the color on a small white card so that you can gauge how much lighter it will become when dry. Add pigment if you desire a more intense color.

This recipe will cover a 20 × 20-foot room. It can be made in quarter and half batches. Do not make more than you need, as the distemper will not keep more than a couple of days.

*Horn or bone glue, available at artist supply stores, is sometimes referred to as "pearl glue" because it comes in little pellets or pearls. An equal amount of rabbit skin glue is an acceptable replacement.

OIL GLAZE

1 egg
2 ounces boiled linseed oil
2 ounces water
No pigment, or just a scant teaspoon

Mix the egg and oil with a whisk, then mix in the water. Glaze is used to modify the look of the painted finish. Depending on how it is mixed, it will either tone down or intensify a painted finish. For example, a clear glaze will soften a look, a touch of green umbra will simulate an aged patina, or a touch of cinnabar will "warm" your wall color. Experiment to find the effect that pleases you most.

Like egg tempera, oil glaze will keep up to three weeks if stored in a tightly covered jar and kept refrigerated. This recipe will cover a small piece of furniture such as a nightstand.

TO DECIDE ON A COLOR SCHEME FOR YOUR INTERIOR, SIT DOWN WITH A COLLECTION OF PAINT CHIPS GATHERED FROM ONE SOFT COLOR SPECTRUM THAT APPEALS TO YOU, FANNING OUT SEVERAL PERMUTATIONS, PERHAPS IN STRAW YELLOW, BLUE-GRAY, OR CELERY GREEN. EXPERIMENT BY JUXTAPOSING SLIGHTLY DIFFERENT VALUES OF THE SAME SHADE. MAKE NOTE OF THE COMBINATIONS THAT MOST PLEASE YOU AND THE DEGREE OF SUBTLETY THAT YOU FIND ATTRACTIVE. ONCE YOU HAVE SELECTED YOUR FAVORITE COLORS, PURCHASE A SMALL AMOUNT—A PINT, IF POSSIBLE—OF EACH ONE YOU CHOSE, THEN PAINT A FEW PATCHES ON THE WALLS AND SEE HOW THEY GROW ON YOU OVER THE NEXT FEW DAYS. LOOK AT THEM IN EVERY LIGHT: DAYLIGHT, LAMPLIGHT, EVEN CANDLELIGHT.

IF YOU ARE ALSO LOOKING FOR FABRIC, BRING YOUR CHIPS TO THE FABRIC STORE AND ASK FOR A SWATCH OF A FABRIC THAT CLOSELY APPROXIMATES THE PAINT CHIPS. (CHECKS AND STRIPES ARE GOOD CHOICES THAT ARE SINGULARLY SWEDISH IN FEELING—SEE "CLASSIC FABRICS," PAGE 61.) TAKE THE SWATCH HOME AND SEE HOW IT REACTS TO THE PAINTED PATCHES ON THE WALL AND TO THE CHANGES OF LIGHT IN YOUR ROOM. WHEN YOU'VE FOUND THE RIGHT COMBINATIONS, YOU'LL BE ABLE TO MAKE YOUR FINAL PURCHASES WITH CONFIDENCE.

SOURCES

Many stores appear in more than one category. For complete information, please refer back to the initial listing.

SWEDISH FABRICS

Country Swedish
(Fabric shown on page 63)
979 Third Avenue, Suite 1409
New York, NY 10022
212-838-1976
800-562-1847
212-838-2372 (fax)
Country Swedish fabrics are available at showrooms throughout the USA. For information call 800-562-1847.

Royal Sweden
(Fabrics shown on page 63)
P.O. Box 174
Short Hills, NJ 07078
201-912-8128

IKEA
(Fabrics shown on pages 62, 63)
For the store nearest you or a catalog, call:
412-747-0747 (East Coast)
818-912-1119 (West Coast)

In Sweden:

Svenskt Tenn
(Fabrics shown on pages 51, 62, 63, 137–38)
Strandvägen, 5
Box 5478
114 84 Stockholm
46-8-670-1600
46-8-660-1468 (fax)

Rand och Ruta (Checks and Stripes)
(Fabrics shown on pages 78, 80, 89)
Kammakargatan, 8#
111 40 Stockholm
46-8-20-40-41
46-8-20-40-41 (fax)

Klässbols Linneväveri
(Fabrics shown on pages 116–19)
Damasvägen, 5
Klässbols, Sweden
46-570-601-85
46-570-604-08 (fax)

Lena Rahoult Fabrics
(Fabrics shown on pages 61, 62)
Nybrogatan, 25
114 39 Stockholm, Sweden
46-8-660-50-30
46-8-661-71-14 (fax)

R.O.O.M.
Alströmergatan 20
Box 49024
S-100 28 Stockholm, Sweden
46-8-651-24-26
46-8-651-26-40 (fax)

COMFORTERS, FEATHERBEDS, AND BEDDING

Chambers
For a catalog, call:
800-334-9790

Cuddledown of Maine
For a catalog, call:
800-323-6793

Dux International/Duxiana
305 East 63rd Street
New York, NY 10021
For the retail store nearest you, call:
212-752-3897
212-319-9638 (fax)

Eddie Bauer
For a catalog, call:
800-426-8020

IKEA

The Company Store
For a catalog, call:
800-285-3696

TABLE LINENS

IKEA

In Sweden:

Klässbols Linneväveri
Svenskt Tenn

SWEDISH CRYSTAL CHANDELIERS

Country Swedish

IKEA 18th Century Collection

In Sweden:

Svenskt Tenn

Titta In
Offers a range of reasonably priced antique crystal chandeliers.
Frejgatan, 14
113 49 Stockholm
46-8-612-84-30

SWEDISH-STYLE BEDS

Country Swedish
(Beds shown on pages 84–85)

Duxiana/Dux Interiors
(Bed shown on page 87)

IKEA
(Bed shown on page 82)

To order a wooden star dowel like the one pictured on page 89, contact Gisela Montan at Rand och Ruta, Stockholm, Sweden, fax #46-8-20-40-41.

FURNITURE (ANTIQUE AND REPRODUCTION)/ ACCESSORIES

Country Swedish

Country Swedish furnishings can also be found at:

Allegria International Ltd.
One Design Center Place
Boston, MA 02210
617-261-4742
617-261-4707 (fax)

Evergreen Antiques
1249 Third Avenue
New York, NY 10021
212-744-5664
212-744-5666 (fax)

IKEA
(Furniture shown on pages 82, 91, 94)

Lars Bolander
5 Toilsome Lane
East Hampton, NY 11937
516-329-3400

Scandina
8 South Madison Street
P.O. Box 2053
Middleburg, VA 20118

The Swedish Blonde Collection
Avancée
30842 Driftwood Drive
S. Laguna Beach, CA 92677
714-499-1865
714-499-3765 (fax)

Victor Antiques
Specializing in Biedermeier.
223 East 60th Street
New York, NY 10022
212-752-4100
212-752-2747 (fax)

In Sweden:

Carl Malmsten AB
Strandvägen, 5B
114 51 Stockholm
46-8-23-33-80
46-8-667-7940 (fax)

Stackelberg Design
590 98 Edsbruk
46-493-503-14
46-493-502-40 (fax)

Svenskt Tenn
(Furniture shown on pages 50, 137–39)

The Swedish Blonde Collection
Avancée
Odinsvägen 37 A
S–130 54 Dalarö
Sweden
46-8501-502-26
46-8501-502-51 (fax)

Tidlös
(Antique wooden horse on page 12)
Roslagsgatan, 17
113 55 Stockholm
46-8-15-30-64

Auction/Antiques/Art

In Sweden:

Antik Mässan
Specializing in antiques and artwork.
Stora Sjötullen
115 25 Stockholm
46-8-662-03-37
46-8-661-16-17 (fax)

Bukowski's
Strandvägen, 7A
Box 1754
111 87 Stockholm
46-8-614-08-00
46-8-611-46-74 (fax)

Glass

Galleri Orrefors
58 East 57th Street
New York, NY 10022
In the United States, call 800-351-9842 for a listing of stores that carry Orrefors crystal.

In Sweden:

Orrefors/Kosta Boda
S-380 40
46-481-340-00
46-481-304-00 (fax)

Wall Coverings

Country Swedish

Spectrum Studio
114 S. Main Street
Lindsborg, KS 67456
913-227-3077

In Sweden:

Svenskt Tenn
Distributes Josef Frank wallpaper designs.

Tile Stoves

Lars Bolander
Will source tiled stoves in Sweden.

Firespaces
U.S. distributors of Cronspisen Swedish Stoves. Will arrange for installation in the home by a certified professional. Call for a catalog.
921 Southwest Morrison, Suite 440
Portland, OR 97205
503-227-0547
503-227-0548 (fax)

Wooden Floors

As an alternative method of bleaching floors, use a prepared kit called "Klean-Strip," available at Home Depot, K-Mart, and Wal-Mart. For additional information, contact:

Klean-Strip
Wm. Barr Co. Inc.
P.O. Box 1879
Memphis, TN 38101-1879
901-775-0100
901-775-5465 (fax)

SWEDISH SPECIALTIES BY MAIL

The smoked codfish roe and herring ingredients listed in the recipe on page 172 can be ordered through many of these companies.

Anderson Butik
Food, gifts, books, and rare items by special order.
P.O. Box 151
Lindsborg, KS 67456
Call for catalog:
800-782-4132

Ducktrap Farms
Smoked salmon available by express delivery.
R.R. 2, Box 378
Lincolnville, ME 04849
800-828-3825
207-763-4235 (fax)

Hemslöd
Accessories, folk crafts, clothing.
P.O. Box 152
Lindsborg, KS 67456
Call for catalog:
800-779-3344
913-227-4234 (fax)

Ingebretsen's
Food, gifts, crafts, cookware, sweaters, books.
1601 East Lake Street
Minneapolis, MN 55407
800-279-9333
612-729-1243 (fax)

Wikstrom's
Swedish foods and cookware.
5247 North Clark Street
Chicago, IL 60640
312-275-6100
312-275-7324 (fax)

ARCHITECTS/DESIGNERS

Jacob Cronstedt
(Work shown on pages 7, 9)
Skeppargatan, 3
114 52 Stockholm
Sweden
46-8-663-9969
46-8-663-1255 (fax)

Jonas Carlsson
Riot AB
Rörstrandsgatan, 30
113 40 Stockholm
46-8-301-272
46-8-329-428 (fax)

Nancy Mullan, ASID, CKD
204 East 77th Street, 1E
New York, NY 10021
(212) 628-4629

Anika Reuterswärd
(Work shown on pages 31, 68, 113, 120–21)
Fogia Collection
Box 5023
141 05 Huddinge, Sweden
46-8-740-8250
46-8-740-76-98 (fax)

DECORATIVE PAINTERS

Björkstads
(Work shown on pages 46, 75)
A team of decorative painters specializing in Swedish painting techniques. Will accept assignments in the United States and Europe.
Kungsklippan, 10
112 25 Stockholm
46-8-652-15-66
46-8-33-31-03 (fax)

Hans Yngve
(Hans Yngve works with the Björkstads group. His work is shown on pages 23, 36, 38, 48, 49, 81)
See Björkstads.

SWEDISH CULTURE

American Scandinavian Foundation
725 Park Avenue
New York, NY 10021
212-879-9779
212-249-3444 (fax)

Consulate General of Sweden/Swedish Information Service
One Dag Hammarskjold Plaza, 45th Floor
New York, NY 10017
212-751-5900
212-752-4789 (fax)
E-mail swedinfo ix.netcome.com
Home page: http://www.sweden info.com/sis

Lindsborg, Kansas
Lindsborg Chamber of Commerce
P.O. Box 191
Lindsborg, KS 67456
913-227-3706

Nordic Heritage Museum
3014 NW 67th Street
Seattle, WA 98117
206-789-5707
206-789-3271 (fax)

SWEA Society
Preserving the Swedish language
124 East 76th Street
New York, NY 10021
212-751-5900
212-752-4789 (fax)

Sweden & America magazine
2600 Park Avenue
Minneapolis, MN 55407-1090
612-871-0593
612-871-8682 (fax)

Swedish-American Museum Center of Chicago
5211 North Clark Street
Chicago, IL 60640
312-728-8111
312-728-8870

The American Swedish Institute
2600 Park Avenue
Minneapolis, MN 55407-1090
612-871-4907
612-871-8682 (fax)
For the American Swedish Institute Bookstore, call:
800-5SWEDEN (800-579-3336)

Embassy of Sweden
1501 M Street NW
Washington, DC 20005
202-467-2600
202-467-2699 (fax)
Home page: http://www.sweden.nw.dc.us/sweden

SWEDISH MUSIC

Phontastic Records
Offers a variety of traditional Swedish music as well as classic and contemporary recordings. For title information and purchases, contact:

Ad Lib
P.O. Box 8332
163 08 Spånga, Sweden
46-8-761-07-65 (fax)

For Phontastic's classic catalog on the Artemis label, contact:

CDA
P.O. Box 4225
106 63 Stockholm
46-8-642-27-75 (fax)

TRAVEL TO SWEDEN AND TOURING

Swedish Travel & Tourism Council
655 Third Avenue, 18th Floor
New York, NY 10017
212-949-2333
212-697-0835 (fax)
Home page: http://travelfile.com/get/swetvl

SAS Airlines
9 Polito Avenue
Lyndhurst, NJ 07071
201-896-3681
201-896-3725 (fax)

DESTINATIONS DESCRIBED IN TEXT

Carl Larsson Garden
790 15 Sundborn
46-23-603-77
46-23-605-53 (fax)

Skansen Open Air Museum
Djurgården
Box 27807
115 23 Stockholm
46-8-442-80-00
46-8-442-82-82 (fax)

The National Museum
S. Blasieholmshamnen
Box 161 76
103 24 Stockholm
46-8-666-4250
46-8-611-37-19 (fax)

SUGGESTED READING

Barwick, JoAnn. *Scandinavian Country.* Clarkson Potter, 1995.
Boman, Monica, ed. *An Orchid in Winter —The Story of Estrid Ericson.* Carlsson Bokförlag, 1989.
Edenheim, Ralph. *Skansen.* Scala Publications, 1995.
Gaymor, Elizabeth. *Scandinavian Living Design.* Stewart, Tabori & Chang, 1987.
Groth, Hakan. *Neoclassicism in the North: Swedish Furniture and Interiors 1770–1850.* Rizzoli, 1990.
Innes, Jocasta. *Scandinavian Painted Decor.* Rizzoli, 1990.
———. *Scandinavian Painted Furniture.* Sterling Publishers, 1991.
Lofgren, John Z., ed. *Carl Larsson; The Autobiography of Sweden's Beloved Artist.* Penfield Press, 1992.
Rydin, Lena. *Carl Larsson Garden, A Home.* Carl Larsson-gården/Dalaförlaget, 1994.
Sjöberg, Lars and Ursula. *The Swedish Room.* Pantheon, 1994.

Many thanks to everyone at Fairfield County Dodge in Norwalk, Connecticut, for the generous loan of the pickup truck shown on page viii.

INDEX